To. Moira
I hope you enjoy reading this.

It's Only a Matter of Time

With my very best wishes.
Robert. 26.8.2012.

Robert J. Montgomery

authorHOUSE®

AuthorHouse™ UK Ltd.
500 Avebury Boulevard
Central Milton Keynes, MK9 2BE
www.authorhouse.co.uk
Phone: 08001974150

First published by AuthorHouse 11/3/2009

ISBN: 978-1-4490-3451-1 (sc)

This book is printed on acid-free paper.

Preface

I was in my teenage years when I realised I was living in an area rich in characters. I feel privileged to have lived amongst such characters, who give this book such a unique diversity of life in this rural area of Fermanagh. I have tried to portray them in as light-hearted a form as I can. The names of some of the characters have been changed to protect their identities.

When my eldest son, Gordon, suggested I should write down some of the stories, anecdotes, history and folklore, I found it easier to relate these in the order in which I had experienced them. As a result this book follows an autobiographical sequence of events from about 1946 and is related as accurately as I can remember. All the characters are real, except those included in the folklore, which are easily identified.

Life in County Fermanagh is changing fast from what I knew as a child. Farming life in those days immediately after the second world war has under gone something akin to a revolution. Gradually the use of the horse, pony, mule, and donkey began to decline, and now the farming industry is heavily mechanised. Using modern machinery, jobs that took two weeks to do in 1960, can now be done in less than one day.

Sadly today, there is a lot less talking and chatting amongst the people. No longer do the young men meet at the local cross-roads for a chat when their day's work is finished. Instead they are driving about in cars, going to the fast food take-away, or meeting in the pubs and clubs of the towns.

Lifestyle is changing so rapidly, it is good to record the old days of hard work, play, and above all contentment. I have included a few mistakes. I'm told that's what people look for!

Contents

The Early Days

Looking back now, I only remember the highlights of those bygone days. I remember clearly the day we took delivery of our President No48 cooker. I was three years old at the time and Mum and Dad had been discussing the purchase of a new cooker for some time. The problem was that we had a chimney that frequently had blow downs when the wind was in a certain direction. This filled the farmhouse kitchen with smoke. Dad said that he had heard a range would stop the problem. The wide chimney breast would be closed in, and just a flue pipe going up, so no down draught would be experienced. On his weekly trip to Enniskillen to collect the groceries for the family, Dad would bring home some brochures of all the latest ranges and stoves, so that he and Mum could discuss which one would be best suited to our situation. Sometimes I looked over the pictures of the ranges and stoves in the glossy pages of the brochures. There were red ones, blue ones, green ones, black ones, and some with Queen Anne legs, which I thought were quite nice. I remember sitting near the open hearth fire, and driving my little matchbox type car along the edge of the bricked hearth, on the concrete floor, and parking into a little pretend garage, just as Dad would have done with the family car outside, and feeling the heat of the peat as it glowed in a gentle blaze on the hearth. Then one day, Mr Chambers who managed the hardware section of J. A. Anderson's, told Dad that a whole new type of cooker was coming on the market, and he would have one in the shop soon. So that was how we got our nice grey enamelled President cooker. It arrived one day in March 1946, and as it weighed about three hundredweight, and hydraulic lifting gear wasn't invented at that time, it had to be man handled down a couple of planks which were placed at the rear of the delivery lorry, and then carried into our kitchen, where it stood against the hall wall for a week, until Granddad Mavitty, and Uncle Ernie came up one night and gave Mum and Dad a hand to lift it up onto the base, which Dad had prepared for it earlier that evening. It worked a treat, no more smoke filled kitchen, a good oven to bake the bread in, and a thick steel top that held the heat which radiated throughout the whole room. Mum was delighted, and always kept it in sparkling condition. About twenty five years later, I was carrying out a renovation to the house and installing hot water. The president cooker wasn't suitable, so I mentioned to Tom Sheridan, who was collecting our milk at that time, that I would have to change it for a different one. Tom said, "I know a man who will buy it off you," and true to his word, he told a man who lived near Swanlinbar about it. The cooker was in lovely condition, and as soon as he saw it he had no hesitation in giving me forty pounds for it. The same figure that had been paid for it originally. How technology had advanced by then. I was able to remove the entire cooker single handed. I used a hydraulic jack to lift the cooker up off the base which I then dismantled.

Next, I lowered the cooker down onto two pieces of steel piping, and rolled it out through the door and onto the tractor link-box, lifted it up by the tractor hydraulics and set it into the purchaser's trailer.

1947, was a year to remember because of the heavy snowfall. There had been small amounts of snow that winter, but one evening towards the end of February the sky darkened down and snow began to fall. I don't remember that but was told later, and next morning I awoke and thought it unusual that I could hear my sisters downstairs talking instead of being off to school. I was still in bed, not having started school yet. I got up, looked out the window and could hardly believe my eyes. Snow had transformed the whole, landscape. The garden hedge, which was about three feet high, was nowhere to be seen, and vast waves of whiteness were everywhere. The snow had been accompanied by a strong wind, which had piled up huge drifts anywhere there were hedges or buildings to obstruct its path. I hurriedly dressed, went downstairs, and outside to see this great event first hand. Dad used the small coal shovel from the house to make a narrow walking path to the tool shed where he got his large navvy shovel to clear a path to the cattle sheds, pig, and poultry houses as the animals would have to be fed, and we could walk along these corridors without getting the cold, wet snow around our feet. Mains water was not yet available in our area, and a normal winter chore, was to letting the cows out two at a time to drink at the well. They were kept in the byre from about November until May each year, and the midday walk was good exercise for them, but this huge snowfall had upset the normal routine of the farm, and Dad had a big task in front of him. He got the early milking, and feeding done, and had taken a back-load of hay to some young stock, which were over-wintering in the lower meadows, where they had a calf shed for shelter. I don't know how other farmers were managing, but Dad used his head and organised us three children with shovels, spades, buckets, or whatever we could use to scoop up the snow and carry it into the boiler house, where a large boiler, normally used to boil potatoes for feeding to the pigs, was kept. We filled it up, Mum lit the fire in the firebox underneath, and soon the snow was melted into water which Dad carried off to the cows. This was good thinking as it fulfilled several necessities and kept us kids warm and happy as we rushed back and forth with shovels of snow to the boiler. Soon the fire was burning well, and as our shovels of snow were dropped into the boiler it melted immediately. So Dad's brain wave worked three ways. Water was provided for the cows. The yard was being cleared of snow, and us kids were having a whale of a time into the bargain. Because we lived about a quarter mile from the main road it was impossible to get the cans of milk out to the roadside for the normal pick up lorry. Our lane-way which was about nine feet wide, with a high hedge running along each side had trapped the snow and was filled level across. Dad used all his spare time, and continued on each night by the light of the moon, until about eleven o'clock, to shovel the snow, and make a walking track down the lane, so we could get out to the main road again. It was hard work but he was a fairly young strong man at that time. I was just four years old and a bit useless when it came to shovelling snow. The topic of the big snow went on for years with tales being told of how the farmers on the high mountain areas such as Marlbank weren't able to get out from their farms for weeks. Uncle Ernie said jokingly afterwards, that he was making his way out the lane on his way to town, through snow that was waist high, when he saw a postman's cap lying on the top of the snow. He went over and lifted it up and, "What do you know," said he, "But wasn't wee George Fawcett the postman looking up at me."

George was the local postman for the Culkey area and a great character also. He lived in the gate house at Rushin near Bellanaleck with his wife Eva. George enjoyed a wee 'howlt' any time he got a chance, and when my Dad's cousin, Elizabeth came from Belfast to our house on holiday he would take her in his arms and land a big kiss on her lips. It was all a bit of fun and I think Elizabeth enjoyed it too. My mother always had a nice warm cup of tea and some bread or scones for George when he delivered the mail to our house which was usually about 9.45 - 10.00 am each day. George told us he was in Johnny McFarland's shop in Enniskillen one day when in came two lovely girls. Johnny gave George a wink and he knew what he meant. George says, "I buckled a howlt of one, while Johnny grabbed the other, and gave them a kiss. What do you think if it wasn't the daughter of your neighbour down the road I had kissed. But she took it in good fun, and just laughed. George and most of his brothers were quite short in stature and my grandfather Mavitty, who was well known for his quick wit, was walking down the street in Enniskillen when he noticed George's brother Johnny walking on the other side. He was after buying some weanling pigs from him a few weeks earlier, so he shouted across to him, "Hello Johnny how are you getting on?" Johnny replied, "The very best, how are the pigs doing, Charlie." "Ah!" says he, "They're like the Fawcett's, they're keeping very small."

Ireland had a lovely sunny summer that year which I suppose was nature's way of making up for the terrible start. The old men always said that a bad month of February would produce a good summer, and certainly 1947 bore that out. September 1948, was the year I started school. All the children started back to school after the summer holidays and for me it was a whole new experience. My mother had asked Victor, the youngest of the Nixon boys, and our nearest neighbour, if he would keep an eye on me. Make sure I was all right, take me to the toilet, and generally look after me. So off I went for my first day of school with my two sisters. We walked down the lane to the Nixon's farmhouse where Victor and Linda were waiting for us. The older ones still at school had gone on already on bicycles or walking. Mrs Nixon had the frying pan on and there was a lovely cooking smell in the house. There were eight children as well as the adults in their house which meant that Mrs Nixon had a servant girl employed to help her with all the chores in the house. Their kitchen window gave a clear view up the road and we had lots of time to walk the last hundred yards down to the road once we saw the school van coming. It was a four wheeled horse drawn wagon, very similar to those we see in Western films. The driver, Mr William Hassard, who lived at Arney, gave us a cheery, "Good morning" as we climbed on board. I sat quietly on the seat along the side as we headed down the road, stopping for John and Victor, the two eldest Elliott boys, at their lane, and then on along to the turn off for the Laragh road where

Kenneth and Gladys Gault got on. After a mile along the Laragh Road we picked up my cousins Ethel and Irene Montgomery, and made the last stop at Gransha for Jim Frazer and Alma Johnston and then proceeded along at a steady walking pace until we reached the school.

The school was a large grey building, standing on an elevated site about fifty yards from the entrance to Lisgoole Abbey, on the Enniskillen to Derrylin road with front and back avenues sweeping up to the front from left and right. After Master Sullivan came to Jones Memorial he planted a laurel hedge along the left side of the front avenue, leaving about three feet of a grass margin between the tarred drive and the laurels. This grass edging was mowed regularly with the lawnmower. The other side of the drive also had the same lawn mowed margin, but the laurels which were spaced at around fifteen feet intervals were clipped into square shapes. All this planting gave the school a nice landscaped appearance. The front elevation had the boys porch to the left which protruded forward by about eight feet from the front wall and was next to a section which was built up into an apex. This was the classroom occupied by Miss Semple who was my first teacher. On the right side, the architectural design was balanced with a similar protrusion which was the girls porch and the Headmaster's house. On the centre of the front wall between two large windows, which had a host of small panes of glass, was a stone plaque inscribed with the words. 'Jones Memorial School erected in 1906.' Victor brought me in through a large heavy door into the boys' porch and helped me to take my coat off which he hung up on one of the hooks, and then brought me through the interior door into the large room where the

7

headmaster taught. The school had three rooms in total. The third room was not in use at this time, but may have been used as a store. Victor left me in the infants class which was taught by Miss Semple. I sat down on a form at the back of the room and listened intently to what was being said. At eleven o'clock the bell was rung, indicating a ten minute break, when we could go to the outside toilet, or eat a snack if hungry. Victor appeared again for me, and took me out through the back playground area and over into the wood where the children were allowed to play, I still remember vividly a huge beech tree which stood on a ridge of ground, just up the bank at the side of the school. Of course, the wood was full of trees, but this one was particularly large and stood out above all the others. The main lunch break came at 1pm. I can't remember what we did in the afternoon, but by 3.30 p.m. we were on our way home again. As we travelled along, Mr Hassard slid open the little hatch between the dickey and the main van, and asked for Bob and Aileen to come out through to him. I crawled out first and then Aileen followed. Aileen was the same age as me and was a beginner also. She was the daughter of our neighbour who lived at Skea Hall, a short distance from our farm if you crossed the fields. I remember Mr Hassard asking me how the first day at school had gone, but I was far too shy to give much of a reply. The horse steadily plodded on and the gravel crunched beneath the steel shoeing on the wheels as we made our way along the Laragh Road (now called the Gransha Road) which was not tarred until 1951. I was intrigued by the twitch of the muscle on his hock as the horse made each step, and the way he swept his tail from side to side to keep the flies off as we proceeded on our homeward journey.

A day or two later, another boy came to school and was placed beside me, he wore a bright red blazer and had fair wavy hair, he was called Albert Crozier, and we soon became friends. A week or so later I made friends with Bobbie Moore, and the three of us are still good friends, some sixty years later. We had some good laughs together and great fun. Some silly phrases were used by us when one of us told a story about someone, another would interject with. 'Ah! sure his father was the same' or 'that's cute.' which later developed into, 'that's extra cute.' Bobbie was always a great character, but always in trouble with the teachers for getting up to some prank or not having his homework done. Bobbie was very intelligent, but didn't bother to use his abilities. Albert, on the other hand was a steady lad who always did his best. I remember Master Sullivan, who taught the senior classes, saying one day that Bobbie was the best in the class at maths. Albert was the best at English, and I was the best all-rounder. We looked forward to the main lunch time break and hurried through our sandwiches so we could get running up through the woods, playing hounds and hares, or in warmer weather have a game of marbles on the concrete bases where nissan huts had once stood when the area was used as a base for the American soldiers during the second world war.

We were out playing hide and seek one lunch time and it was Bobbie's turn to find us. I was up the wood hiding behind a big beech tree when I noticed lumps, like warts, sticking out of the tree bark. I would normally have listened quietly and as Bobbie went by I would have eased myself around to the other side of the tree so he wouldn't have seen me, but on this occasion I was so engrossed with the lumps on the tree, that I failed to hide myself. He spotted me and shouted, "One, two, three, Robert Montgomery looking up the big beech tree." When we were about nine or ten years old and it was getting near to Christmas, Bobbie said there was no such person as Father Christmas, but Albert was a firm believer, and was not very pleased with Bobbie's remark and told him to not come out with the like of that again. I, on the other hand didn't know what to make of Bobbie's statement because Santa had always brought me toys and presents at Christmas, and how could he not exist, sure it was very confusing and just made no sense. For me, school in the 1950's was a place you were sent against your will, and the teacher was very quick to use the cane for the slightest misconduct, or wrong answer in class. School I think was too strict then, but is now too lenient.

At that time Miss Semple was the teacher for infants, 1st, 2nd, and 3rd, classes, and boy! her cane could leave the hands smarting if you were unfortunate enough to get less than seven spellings right out of ten. I fell foul to this on a few occasions as spelling was always my worst subject. At the end of second class she said to me, "My boy, you're going to get plenty of the cane this year." I worried and fretted as to why I was going to be caned on a regular basis, as I had got very good marks in that years exams. But it didn't really materialise, and I gradually ceased to fear her threat. It was years later before I figured out her thinking. She thought that giving me plenty of the cane would mean a sustained good result. When I was young I found it hard to see the meaning in poetry, but Miss Semple had us learn off some poems that I can still remember in parts. 'The Village blacksmith,' and

Wordsworth's famous one about the daffodils, but the one I most enjoyed was the one by Lewis Carroll called 'Father William.' I believe it was a parody of an earlier poem by Robert Southey. 'The Old Man's Comforts.'

Father William

"You are old Father William," the young man said,
 "And your hair has become very white,
and yet you incessantly stand on your head,
do you think at your age it is right?"
"In my youth," Father William replied to his son,
"I feared it might injure my brain,
but now that I'm perfectly sure I have none,
why I do it and do it again."
"You are old," said the youth, "as I mentioned before,
and have grown most uncommonly fat,
yet you turned a back somersault in at the door,
pray, what is the reason of that?"
"In my youth," said the sage, as he shook his grey locks,
"I kept all my limbs very supple
by the use of this ointment, one shilling a box,
allow me to sell you a couple."
"You are old," said the youth," and your jaws are too weak
for anything tougher than suet,
yet you finished the goose, with the bones and the beak,
pray, how did you manage to do it?"
"In my youth," said his father, "I took to the law,
and argued each case with my wife,

and the muscular strength which it gave to my jaw,
has lasted the rest of my life."
"You are old," said the youth, "one would hardly suppose,
that your eye was as steady as ever,
yet you balanced an eel on the end of your nose,
what made you so awfully clever?"
"I have answered three questions, and that is enough,"
said his father, "don't give yourself airs!
Do you think I can listen all day to this stuff?
Be off or I'll kick you down stairs!"

As life went on and I moved to the higher classes, I developed a respect for Miss Semple. I began to understand her use of the cane. She was trained to think that the fear of getting the cane, would force the children to have all their work completed, and as well done as possible,..... maybe it did work! The daily routine of, get up, washed, dressed, have breakfast, and walk the four hundred yards, or so, to the main road with my school books in a leather bag on my back soon became normal life for me. But it was always great to look forward to Saturdays, when I could have some fun, or go with John Hassard the farm worker, to enjoy watching him work, and chat with him. Like everybody else, John had great ideas about how the country should be run and how he would do it. I remember asking him, why were there world wars, and he said it was for more territory, a word I didn't understand at the time.

Some time later the number of school pupils had increased

to over one hundred, and the third room was brought into use. A new teacher, Miss Bussell, was employed. I think she may have been out from college on training practice, because she left after a short time to be replaced by Miss Crawford who taught the beginners at the old school and continued when the school was replaced with a new building at Mullylogan. While in one of the lower classes, I was asked to read a paragraph by Miss Bussell. I eventually came to a word which was new to me, so I stopped. Miss Bussell said, "again," so back I went to the beginning, and read along until I came to the same unpronounceable word, and there I stopped, Miss Bussell said "again," so back I went to the beginning again, and had just got restarted when Miss Bussell interrupted with, "Robert, the word is again."

Two years before I left primary school another teacher was employed. His name was Roy Palmer. He taught classes 4th and 5th in one half of the large classroom. He was a strict, well dressed, athletic young man with his light brown hair combed back, and the toe-caps of his black shoes polished until they shone like mirrors. I was never in his class, but he did take our class occasionally for physical education in the yard behind the school. My friend Bobbie fell foul of him one day as the school was breaking up for the summer holidays. We were on the bus at the school gate, and Mr Palmer was standing alongside supervising our safe departure. He looked up at the window where Bobbie was sitting. Bobbie thought he was in a safe location and shook his fist at him. "Report to me after the holidays boy," he bellowed. Poor Bobbie later told me he did no good for the entire eight weeks of the holidays, wondering what would happen when school restarted in September. Sure enough, he remembered the incident and gave Bobbie lines to write as a punishment.

A lot of schools have tuck-shops and though we had none we were privileged to have a small shop across the road and up past Culkey Post Office. It was run by Mr Tom Walsh and his daughter Lilah. Having a 'sweet-tooth,' I went there as often as my pocket money allowed. The master had to check if you had money before you were allowed to go. The little shop was part of their house and a few pence would buy a liquorice pipe, a sherbet fountain, or six pence for a bar of milk chocolate. I remember Bobbie saying to Albert and I, after he had purchased some chocolate, "Come on boys and help me dismantle this bar of chocolate." We helped very willingly!

Miss Semple was a great singer, and took the music class each week, and that was not without some incidents. To get our pitch right, we first sang up and down the 'Tonic Sol-fa.' She would hit her tuning fork off the table and announce with fervour, "You're are as flat as pancakes." We would then progress on to a piece, something like, 'Ye banks and brae's O'Bonny Doon,' she would stop us at every note that was not in tune, or pitched too low, as was the norm. One day, she went through a piece of music, explaining all the signs, marks, dynamics, and what they meant. At the end of the piece were two letters, 'D.C'. She asked the class if any of us knew what they meant. Hugh Abercrombie quickly shot up his hand, and when she said "yes," he answered, "Please Miss, Dick Cutler." He was promptly sent to the Headmaster for a caning. Dick was one of our class mates. Around about that same time, a new hall was erected at Bellanaleck, and the school choir was asked to come and sing at a concert there. Miss Semple selected two pieces for us to sing, "The Isle of Innisfree", and "How much is that doggie in the window." We practised hard and did all Miss Semple asked of us. Then one day while we were rehearsing, Master Sullivan came into the room to hear us. When we finished he said, "You won't be heard past the second row, come on and put a bit of power into it." We sang it again at a good coarse shout, and he said, "That's more like it." After he left the room, Miss Semple said, "That's exactly what I don't want you to do, you should always sing as sweetly as possible and I guarantee that you will be easily heard at the back of the hall." Some advice I have never forgotten. The big night arrived, and I remember the nervous tension as we made our way onto the stage. We sang 'The Isle of Innisfree' first, and the audience gave us a rapturous applause, and then we did, 'The doggie in the window.' John Sheridan was appointed to do the 'bark-bark' at a couple of places, as he was the best at making the doggie sounds. Well, the boys at the back of the hall joined in, and soon there were dogs barking all over the place. However it did go down well, and again a great applause when we finished. My Mother said we were the best item there, but then Mums are usually biased.

Two highlights of our week in the senior school, taught by Master Sullivan, were Tuesday and Friday afternoons. That was when the girls had knitting or hand work class on the Tuesdays and cookery class on the Fridays, and us boys had horticulture both days. So out we would go, and depending on the season, we could be setting up vegetable beds, or digging the ground, or tidying up around the school. It was great to be selected to mow the lawns. Master Sullivan had a large cylinder mower with a small wooden roller at the front and a large steel roller at the back, and he put two of us to the task of lawn-mowing. He had a rope with each end attached to the front of the mower so that one of us could put it over our heads and under our armpits and pull, while the other one pushed, and steered it along. I remember Albert and I enjoying doing this chore on many an occasion. The big bonus was usually in September or October when the strawberries had finished fruiting, and had put out new runners, Master Sullivan would cut these off, and give each of us some to take home to plant in our own gardens. Of course, no one liked having to weed, but we could cover the entire area very quickly because there were usually about fifteen to twenty of us, and each one had only a small section to do. There was many an unhappy day in Master Sullivan's class. If the mood was bad, he would cane us for the slightest thing. I remember getting it a few times, but there were some in my class who seemed to get caned every day. I used to feel sorry for them, as they just didn't have much academic abilities, and it wasn't their fault that they couldn't do the work. There was one boy in the senior class who was excellent at maths, but useless at English. Master Sullivan was always caning him. However, one day the lad decided he would give the Master some of his own medicine, and when he came down with the cane on his hand, he caught it, whipped it from the Master, and gave him two or three good wollops with it, saying, "How do YOU like it!" That ended the caning, but the lad may as well have stayed at home afterwards as he was just ignored in the class. When Master Sullivan was in good humour things were so different and everybody was happy. I remember one day when he was doing geography with us, which was my favourite subject, he got carried away with a story about how the British defeated the French at the heights of Abraham in Quebec. To further clarify the topic he threw himself down on the floor to show us how a soldier falls when he is shot. Down he went full whack, knocking his head, which took a loud ring out of the iron heating pipes that ran close to the floor, around the walls of the room. We had very little sympathy for him, and had trouble keeping from laughing as he moaned and rubbed his aching head. That concluded the insight on warfare, and the geography lesson ended in a more sombre mood.

My mother told me of an exploit of her brother Leslie, who was taught at Jones Memorial during the period when Master Borrows was the headmaster. Leslie was going home from school one day when along came a farmer called Simon Sands with his pony and cart. As they made their way along the road, Leslie started to chant, Simy - Simy - Sulphur - Simy. "I'll report you to the headmaster you cheeky rascal," threatened Mr Sands. Sure enough, next day Mr Sands went down to the school, and told Master Burrows that young Mavitty had called him names on his way home from school on the previous evening. "What did he call you?" asked Master Burrows. "He called me Simey - Simey - Sulphur - Simey." he replied. The master doubled in two laughing and Mr Sands stumped off disgusted, and mumbling to himself, "you're as bad as he is." Mr Sands had a daughter called Florrie and I heard a good anecdote about her. Her neighbour, Christy Graham, took a fancy to Florrie, and decided he would like to marry her. But before that, he had to tell his widowed mother what he had in mind. So one day he plucked up courage and said to his widowed mother. "Did you hear that Florrie Sands is going to get married?" "No," she replied, "Who is she going to marry?" "Me," said Christy.

The years were passing by, and the horse drawn wagon had long since been replaced with a modern school bus. The Nixon's, and my sisters had finished with school, Aileen's family had sold their farm to the McCullagh family. Evelyn McCullagh, Cyril Geddes, and myself, were the only children now attending Jones Memorial primary school who caught the bus at Derrygiff lane. Cyril was a few years younger than me and we would have interesting boy-chats about how to make a good bow and arrow, or catapult, as we waited for the bus. Evelyn, on the other hand would not talk to us, but used to park herself in a little track on the bank under a big chestnut tree and ignore us. Evelyn was in the same class as me, and would talk to me at every opportunity in class, but waiting for the bus...... not a cheep.

My last year at primary school was under a new headmaster, Mr Whittaker. He was the fourth person to hold that post. The first and second were both called Burrows, Mr Sullivan being the third. Mr Whittaker had a different style of teaching and was not as erratic as Mr Sullivan. I had still a year to do at school, and intended to stay at home on the farm when I finished school, so I had not gone forward for the exams to second level education. Mr Whittaker suggested some of us should do the Leaving Certificate, and the Technical examination. Another friend of mine, Cecil Phair, said he would do the exams if I did.

We both did the exams and passed, so the next term saw me at the Technical School, where I met up again with my friend Bobbie who had gone there a year earlier. Bobbie was still full of fun and as carefree as ever. Although he was in a different class, we met in the dining hall each day for lunch. Bobbie used to volunteer for the job of server, he said you could get extra helpings that way. I soon learned that dinners in the 'tech' had to be eaten fast or you could miss out on sweet or seconds. The first day at the Technical school was so different from the more colloquial atmosphere of Jones Memorial. Cecil and I were in the same class and during the first break period we decided to take a stroll up the town and get some sweets. This was a very lucky thing for us, as we later discovered, the older boys were waiting for all the new boys to go to the toilets where they had the wash basins full of cold water, and several of them would take the new comers and dip their heads in the water. This came to our attention when we returned to the classroom and saw our classmates there with wet heads. Apparently this was an initiation ceremony for the new boys. Now that we knew the procedure, Cecil and I avoided getting a ducking. I found there always seemed to be someone in the class who stood out as a leader, and IC, my class, was no different, so when it came time to elect our form Prefect, we elected the greatest rascal in the class.

Cecil and I were sitting together for our first day in the English class awaiting the arrival of our teacher. He turned out to be a middle aged, grey-haired man, with a quarter inch of stubble on his face. He had a run from his nose going down his top lip, and wore an old badly fitting jacket. Altogether an un-cared for, rough looking character. He sat down at his desk and announced in a nasal tone. "Right boys, get out your Black Arrows." The 'Black Arrow' was a text book he used to explain the English grammar. Cecil whispered to me, "This lad appears to be very easy on razor blades." I gave a giggle and the teacher heard me. Turning to look in my direction he said, "Silly giggling is a sign of stupidity."

In complete contrast, we had a great maths teacher, Mrs Benson. She was fair and firm with us, and we moved quickly through the curriculum, and were soon doing algebra and solving equations. I had a big disadvantage in that I had never learned anything about algebra at primary school, whereas the other boys seemed to have a basic understanding of it. I could not see how, or know when to move my values across the equal sign, and thought of asking Mrs Benson, if she would give me some private tuition, so I could understand what I was supposed to do. But I could never pluck up the courage to ask her. Instead I decided to leave the Technical School, because my father had just purchased a new tractor, and it had a very strong appeal to me. I used to stand and look at it for hours, studying every nut and bolt and memorising the layout of the pipe-work of the big diesel engine. I was very proud of that Ferguson 35. It was the first tractor on the local market to have a cushioned seat and I couldn't wait to get using it on the farm. I went along to Mr Hanna, the Principal, and told him I was leaving the school. I remember him suggesting I do an agriculture course, and said I was only able to cut thistles with my present abilities. He finally said he would be in touch with my father, but he never did. So ended my school days.

Of course another type of school, Sunday School, had ended also as I was now fifteen years old, and had become a full member of our local Methodist Church at Mullaghy. Sunday school was such a pleasant event compared to day school. My sisters, and I would get dressed up in our best clothes immediately after our mid-day meal, and meet up with the Nixon girls, and the Elliotts, our other neighbours who lived just across the fields in the opposite direction to the Nixon's farm. All of us walked the mile or so down the road to the church, calling in at Miss Price's house for the Church key. Her niece, Miss Taylor always greeted us with a laugh, and I thought she was one of the jolliest people I had met in my young life. Sometimes we were too early for Sunday school, and Miss Taylor would invite us in to wait until the teachers, Mr and Mrs Johnston, came along in their car. The Sunday school had about twenty members when I started, including my cousins, the Montgomery's from Gransha, and John and Albert Wallace from Oakfield. Mrs Johnston took the Juniors while Mr Johnston took the seniors. I remember Mrs Johnston making me so welcome in her sincere and kindly way. The Sunday school opened with the singing of a hymn, then Mr Johnston led in prayer, and then we divided into two groups. Mrs Johnston would read a suitable passage of scripture from the Bible, and then explain the meaning to us. I remember her reading the story of Samuel, and on another day telling us the meaning of the rainbow, and how God had promised it as a sign that he would never again destroy the earth with a flood. The highlight of our year was the Sunday school outing to Bundoran every Summer. Mrs Johnston would arrange for a bus to take us there, and also arrange a meal, usually in the Shell House Café. Having got a good tuck in, I would head off with my cousins, John, Albert, and Willie, to the 'dodgems,' (or bumping cars as we called them) and perhaps have a milk-shake, in between trips, but all this was very sore on the pocket money, and when all was spent we would go down to the beach and kick football. Sometimes our families rounded us up for evening tea, and maybe after that we would do a walk along the cliffs known as 'Rougey,' before heading back to the bus. Then we all settled down in the bus for the thirty miles journey home, it was all over for another year.

I never thought that I would be back at the Technical School again, but I was wrong. A couple of years later, I decided to go to the farm machinery maintenance evening class, which was held there for two hours per week. I went with the thought that I could learn how to do electric welding, and be able to do my own farm machinery repairs. When I got there, I found that a lot of other young farmers had a similar idea, which meant the welder was kept very busy, and training limited. I did get a couple of lessons, and soon picked up the skill. I noticed that a lot of the lads were making link-boxes for their tractors, but I had one already, so I decided a hedge trimmer would be a handy machine on the farm. My father thought I would never be able to construct something like that so I explained to him what I had in mind. I got myself an old scrap horse mowing machine which I dismantled and used some of the steel shafts for mounting my drive pulleys. I used the finger bar for my trimmer and shortened the driving rod so that I could rotate the finger bar in a one hundred and eighty degree circle, allowing me to cut at all necessary angles. I then made a frame to fit on the tractor three point linkage and fitted my finger bar on the end of an eight foot piece of strong steel piping which I had connected at right angles to the linkage frame. This gave me the height and reach required for the varying height and shapes of the hedges. I had just the old mower blade to cut the hedge but I found it was sufficiently strong for one year's growth on the hedges. I was able to raise and lower the boon with some chains and the tractor hydraulics. My prototype had a few hiccups at the start. I remember the long driving belt vibrated wildly but I was able to solve that problem by fitting two small jockey pulleys midway along the belt. My machine was able to cut the hedges as I had planned and I was very proud of my achievement.

Uncle Tom

Being the only boy in the family has its good and bad points. First of all, you are pampered or perhaps over protected, at least that's how I remember feeling as a very young boy growing up on the family farm at Derrygiff. There was the problem of having two older sisters who were more interested in knitting than coming out to play football with me. So I had to largely find my own things to do as though I was an only child. I did have one ally however, that maybe a lot of other boys in the same sort of predicament did not have, and that was old Uncle Tom. He was actually my Father's Uncle, and therefore my great-uncle, but all the family called him Uncle Tom.

Uncle Tom was a fairly small man, of a light build, with a big moustache, and a liking for a wee glass of whiskey from time to time. He was also a great storyteller, as were a lot of people of his generation.

An uncle of mine once told me a story about Tom, which made me think he could be quite irresponsible at times. He told me that when Tom was a young man he sometimes took a walk down the road with one of his friends. On one particular summer's evening, they had got as far as the turn off for the Gransha Road when they heard the sound of a horse and trap coming along the road from the Enniskillen direction. As it came closer they could hear men singing party songs. Now feeling was running high in Ireland at that time, with talk of Home Rule. You were either for it, or against it, and these fellows coming along the road were not singing the songs Tom and his friend liked to hear. Tom said to his friend, "It's those boys from up the road, come on we'll give them a bit of a hiding, cut a couple of ash plants, and we'll hide in those bushes." He told his friend to keep hidden until he called for him. By this time, the pony and trap with four strong young fellows were almost level with them. Then Tom jumped out and grabbed the pony by the head, bringing it to a halt, and immediately started lashing the startled youths with his ash plant as hard as he could. Seeing it was a lone attacker the boys were about to overpower him when Tom shouted, "Come on the rest of you and give me a hand." This was the pre-arranged cue. Immediately his friend jumped out yelling and lashing all around him with his ash plant in a real frenzy. Thinking they had landed into a large ambush, the boys gave their pony a crack of the whip and galloped off up the road as fast as they could go. Tom and his friend had many a good laugh when telling the story later, but it could have had a different ending had the boys realised there were only the two of them, and not a whole gang as they had imagined. This sort of incident was quite common at that time as there were always fights going on between the rival parties.

Tom had an early influence on my life, that I only heard of years later. My Mother told me that when I was born, Tom said I should be called Robert, after my Grandfather who had died twelve years before that.

Uncle Tom left the family home at Derrygiff as a young man to make his own way in the world. He spent a few years in Canada where he worked on the construction of the Canadian - Pacific Railway, but he decided to return to Ireland and worked in the docks at Belfast for most of his life, returning home to Derrygiff after he retired. While still quite active, he would make his way by bus into Enniskillen and get a couple of glasses of his favourite beverage, and then buy some fresh herrings, of which he was also very fond. While on one of these trips to town he was standing at a corner, passing the time until the home going bus was ready to leave, when a policeman came along and told him to move along. Tom was not a man to be pushed around and refused to budge, whereupon the policeman reached out to manually move him. But he had underestimated our Tom, who made a quick swing with his fist, and before the policeman could get a grip of him, he caught him on the chin with an uppercut, knocking him to the ground. It was time to make a hasty retreat, so Tom nipped up a side street at top speed. When the cop recovered, he blew his whistle for help, but Tom was well away and out of sight by this time. The policeman had no idea which way he had gone, so Tom got clean away.

I remember one sunny day when I was about five years old, Uncle Tom took me by the hand and said, "Come on Robert we'll go out for a walk," so out we went down the lane. We walked slowly along until Uncle Tom said, "Maybe we have gone far enough, I think we should turn round and go back home." Tom was seventy years older than me, and probably thought the return journey, which was uphill, would be enough for him to walk that day. Eventually we got back to the farmyard again and sat down in the sunshine on some concrete blocks that my father had got to build a new stable for the horse. These were stacked close by the turf house. Some of them were quite low so Uncle Tom and I could sit down, rest, and enjoy the sunshine. He lit his pipe, and then after a few comforting puffs, he commenced to tell me of things that had happened in the past, which on reflection now, I would class as being from a vivid imagination, but he told me in all seriousness. He said, "Do you see that big ash tree," pointing with his pipe in his hand, to a large tree beside the gate into our front field. "There used to be a pot of gold there at the butt of it, and another one round at the back of the hay-shed." I was only five years old, but I said back to him, "Where are they now?" and he replied, "Ah now! that's not for me to say, but there are people not far away who know." As well as his pipe and plug of tobacco, he also carried a small bar of metal in his jacket pocket. It was about four to five inches long, and about half an inch square, which he told me was bullion. I think it was either a bar of lead or solder as it was soft and silver in colour, but to him it was gold bullion.

On another day, he told me that as a young man he was going to Bellanaleck, and the shortest way to walk there was across the fields to Skea Hall, and then over the meadows near to Nixon Hall. (Which was an old mansion in ruins at that time.) As he was passing by a large beech tree, a wee man stepped out from behind it and bid him, "good evening," and they got into a great chat, whereupon he invited him into his house for a cup of tea. Well, story followed story until Tom realised it was getting late, and he would have to be on his way. "No such thing," said the wee man, "You can stay here for the night." Tom, realising it was useless to argue, agreed to stay, but the house was so very small that it had only one room and only one bed. The wee man said, "My wife will get in first and lie near to the wall, I will get in the middle, and you can sleep at the outside, but before we sleep we will each tell a story," and said to his wife, "You tell yours first Lizzie. " He told his story next, and when he had finished he said to Tom," It's your turn now." "But I have no story to tell," responded Tom. Immediately the wee man kicked him out of bed saying, "You'll have a story to tell after this," and then he woke up and found himself lying at the bottom of the same beech tree.

Ireland has long been known for it's leprechauns, fairies and people with the black art, and Uncle Tom was a firm believer in all these things. He reckoned there were people who could cast a sort of spell, and could take away the milk from your cows, if you were to get on the wrong side of them. He recalled how on May day morning (1st May) this fellow who evidently had 'the black art' went around the local dairy farms in the early morning before the owners were out of bed, and would call out, "Come all to me…. come all to me," and the milk ran out of his boots!

In his later years, Uncle Tom spent a lot of time sitting on the couch in the kitchen, sometimes reading the newspaper, listening to the radio, or talking to Mother as she went about her daily household tasks. After we came home from school one day, Mother was all smiles and in a very happy, jovial mood and couldn't wait to get pointing out to us the new look Uncle Tom had given himself. He had developed a small lump or pimple on his eyebrow and decided to scratch it. His nails weren't giving him any satisfaction, so he took an old safety razor blade out of his waistcoat pocket and proceeded to scrape his eyebrow with it to get rid of the pimple. The end result was that he shaved his eyebrow off completely, and looked really odd, with only one bushy eyebrow. Every time Mother looked at him she burst out laughing, and laughed even more when Uncle Tom crossly asked, "What are YOU laughing at !"

I had many a pleasant day listening to Uncle Tom and his stories but eventually his health started to decline. He developed bronchitis and his breathing got very laboured. My Father and Mother used sit up at night with him, thinking that he wouldn't see the next morning, but he struggled on. Then Uncle Robbie suggested that he and his cousin Tom, would give Mum and Dad a break. They came to sit with him for a night while Mum and Dad got some sleep. Tom and Robbie were sitting in the farmhouse kitchen, chatting quietly with the door open into the room in which old Uncle Tom was lying, when they suddenly realised the laboured breathing and moaning had stopped, all was quiet, not a sound from Uncle Tom, so they moved quietly into the room to see if he was all right. After a little while Tom said to Robbie, "I'm afraid he's gone," whereupon old Uncle Tom said, "Ah! naw, naw, naw." He eventually recovered and lived for another three years after that.

The end finally came when I was nine years old. Uncle Tom was a small man but now his body had got very thin and he probably weighed little more than five stones, his lungs were congested with bronchitis making his breathing very difficult and Mum and Dad knew he couldn't last much longer. The morning he died, he asked my Mother to give him two boiled eggs for breakfast as he was feeling very hungry. She did as he asked and a little later he called for me. I was at home from school with a cold that day and was still upstairs in bed when I heard him calling me from his bedroom downstairs. He wanted me to help him out to the commode. My father was in the house at the time and he went to him and lifted him out. Dad had no sooner sat him on the commode when he said, "I'm dying," and slumped over dead. It was the first funeral I remember, and I couldn't understand how some people were chatting away in a happy sort of way when I thought everybody should have been sad. For after all my Great Uncle Tom was gone, and we would all miss him.

The Band

I was coming home on the bus one evening, having been only one week at the Technical school, when I was approached by a couple of other lads of my own age to join the band. Mullaghy Flute Band was established in the late eighteen hundreds to lead the Orangemen on their annual parade, and celebration day which is held on the twelfth of July each year. Everybody from the whole community went along to the venue, to either join in the large parade, which usually took over an hour to pass a given point, or just to stand along the route, and enjoy the spectacle of all the colourful regalia, and banners of each lodge, led by bands playing music on Flutes, Accordions, Bagpipes, or Brass, which gave the whole thing a lovely 'Carnival' atmosphere. On arrival home I told my parents that David, and some other boys wanted me to join the band, and to come along to the practice in Gransha Hall on Friday evening at eight o'clock, to which my father replied. "That's all right if you want to join, but if you do join, then stay with it, and don't be leaving in a year or so, like so many of the young ones do."….I joined and stayed for fifty years.

So off I went to my first band practice, and met up with about twelve other new recruits. Mr Vaughan, a man of medium build with dark hair, but going bald on top, had a very striking feature, which was a large gingery moustache. He had retired from the police force, and had volunteered to teach us, even though he didn't play the flute himself, he was conversant with music generally. We started by blowing into the flute. A lot of people were having difficulty in achieving the desired sound, but I had no problem as I had been playing from about the age of seven on an old flute that was in our house. I used to play, Onward Christian Soldiers, Stand up Stand up for Jesus, and a few other tunes by ear. George Fawcett, our postman, was also the trainer of the main band, and he often heard me on the old one keyed flute when he called at our house to deliver the mail. He said to me, "You'll have to join the band young fellow. I have an 'F' flute at home and I will bring it round to you some day." This statement was repeated from time to time over the next five or six years, until that first night at the hall. When us beginners were finished with Mr Vaughan, the members of the main band arrived. George welcomed me there and immediately said, "I'll bring you that 'F' flute the next night." I had thought by this time that I would never see the flute, but sure enough on the next Friday night, in came George with the 'F' flute, which I played for the next forty years, until the band got a set of new modern silver flutes in 1996.

The band room in those early days was cold, especially on a cold, frosty, winter's night, so a large gas heater was purchased to ease the problem. It was suspended from the ceiling and had quite a purr from it as it glowed red above our heads. We arrived one night and the cylinder was out of gas, after having been left turned on since our last meeting. Mr Vaughan was furious, because the hall was so cold, and demanded to know which of us had left the gas turned on, but no one admitted to doing it. His glare went from one to the next until he looked at me. Immediately I blushed up from ear to ear. He said, "I think I know who did it," and there I was completely innocent, but convicted by my shyness.

I enjoyed the band, there was always good chat, and the occasional yarn from Bertie. Bertie was one of the drummers, and his jokes, of which he seemed to have an endless supply, gave us all a good laugh. One night, I was going home along with David and Eric, and carrying David Hassard on the crossbar of my bicycle. We stopped to let David off the crossbar at the end of his lane when we heard a slight shuffling sound nearby. I immediately shone my bicycle lamp in the direction of the sound, and there was what appeared to be a couple leaning up against the gate pillar, my lamp clearly picking out a long white leg. I switched off the light and whispered, "It's a courting couple." We all moved on a bit further and stopped to consider how David was going to get past them to go up his lane. But before we could devise a plan, footsteps started coming towards us .I switched on my light again, and there was Bertie, and his friend Ivan. They had decided to play a trick on us younger ones on the way home that night, by pretending they were a courting couple, and sure enough our imaginations had supplied the necessary ingredient to complete the scenario.

We had a lengthy stand at the end of David's lane one other night. Ivan was cycling with us on our return from the band as usual when he started to tell us an old Irish tale, which we thought was going to go on forever, but eventually it did reach a conclusion. He started by telling us that over at Bellanaleck there were three men called, Hudden, Dudden, and Peter Maguire. Now Peter was a successful small farmer. Hudden, and Dudden, had farms too, and although they tried their best, they just couldn't match Peter's skills, abilities, or intelligence, so a jealously developed. One day Hudden said to Dudden. "We'll have to do something about Peter Maguire," so they and connived a plan to spoil his prosperity. The next night when Peter was sleeping, Hudden and Dudden came quietly to his house and killed his best bullock. On seeing this next morning Peter thought, what will I do. Soon a thought came to him, he skinned the dead beast and cut up the carcass for meat to feed his family. When he had dried the pelt he set off one day to Enniskillen to sell it, hoping it might fetch a shilling at the tannery. It was a fine sunny day and Peter rolled up the pelt and slung it over his back in a rope and had nearly reached the town when he decided to sit down by the side of the road to rest. After a while a Magpie came over and started to peck at the pelt. Peter watched for a while, and when the magpie came close enough he quickly reached out his hand and caught it. He tied it's legs, and put it into his large inside pocket, thinking to himself that maybe someone would buy it from him in town later. He made his way to the tannery in Gaol Street, (Belmore Street now) and sure enough he got a shilling for the bullock's pelt. The next thing was to get something to eat, so off he went to a cheap eating house and ate his fill. Then he started to think that someone here might buy the magpie which was still in his pocket, so he pulled it out and set it up on the table with it's legs still tied. A man came over to him and asked what he was doing with the magpie. Oh! said Peter, "I have it for sale." "Well no one is going to buy it here, sure you could get as many as you want for nothing." "Ah! But this is no ordinary magpie," said Peter, "This magpie can talk, and I reckon it's worth a lot of money." "A lot of rubbish," said the man, "Sure everybody knows that magpies can't talk," "I'll have you to know that I can talk," said the magpie. The man was utterly astounded, and seeing the potential, immediately said, "I'll give you a shilling for that bird," "Not likely," said Peter. In no time at all a crowd had gathered, and soon they were outbidding each other for the bird. When it reached ten shillings, Peter thought it was enough and sold it to a very happy man. Of course he didn't know that Peter had taught himself the gift of ventriloquism and had spoken on behalf of the bird.

A couple of days later, Hudden, and Dudden could hardly believe their eyes when they saw Peter out ploughing a field with a new team of oxen which he had purchased with his money from the sale of the magpie. They went over to him, curious to know how he had managed to buy the two oxen. "Oh!" said Peter, "Someone killed my best bullock, but I skinned it off and sold the pelt in town for ten shillings." "Man dear that's a powerful price for a pelt," said Dudden," and turning to Hudden, he said, We should kill our two and sell their pelts." So the next day Hudden, and Dudden killed the two and only bullocks that they had, dried the pelts, and headed for town to get the big money. But all they could get was one shilling per pelt. Hudden and Dudden came home very sad. What could they do now. They had two shillings, no bullocks, not enough money to buy some more, and worst of all Peter Maguire had hoodwinked them into killing their own bullocks.

This was it, Maguire would have to go. So they spent that night laying a careful plan as to how they would deal with him. Next morning, they arrived at Peter Maguire's house, where they lay in wait until he came out. Hudden grabbed him while Dudden pulled a large sack over his head, and tied it tight. Poor Peter was taken completely by surprise, and powerless to do anything. They carried him off intending to dump him into the Arney river at Drumane, but they got tired carrying him and left him down near the bridge, and went into the house of a friend nearby for some tea to calm themselves down, after all they had done a lot of badness in their life, but as yet they had never murdered anyone. While they were in the house a farmer came along the road, driving a herd of cattle. He noticed the sack lying by the roadside, and wondered what could be in it. He undid the string and said to Peter, "What on earth are you doing in there." "To be perfectly honest I was having a most amazing experience," said Peter, "The wind passing through the sack produces the most beautiful sound, almost like an Angel playing a harp." "Get out of there and let me hear that," asked the farmer, to which Peter gladly agreed. As soon as he got into the sack Peter quickly tied it up, and went off home taking the farmers cattle with him. Very soon Hudden, and Dudden reappeared and took the sack, carried it the last bit, and chucked it over the bridge into the river, despite the shouts of protest from inside the bag, and then went on their way content that they had got rid of Peter Maguire once and for all.

Hudden arose bright and early next morning, and there before his eyes he saw twelve cattle grazing on Peter Maguires field. He went over to Dudden's house and told him what he had seen. "Come on," said Dudden, "Let's go over and get a closer look." They arrived at the house and when they saw Peter they thought they were seeing a ghost, and went as white as a sheet. "We threw you into the river yesterday," said Hudden, "How did you get out of the sack, and where did you get all those cattle?" "I was very fortunate," said Peter, "The current swept me downstream, and the sack caught on a very sharp rock that was jutting out from the river bank, tearing it open, I worked my way free, and there on my right was a huge cave. I swam over to it and went inside, and started up the slope out of the water. I didn't go very far when light began to appear, so I kept on going, and what do you think, if I didn't come across a huge herd of cattle, maybe a hundred head sheltering in the cave. I tried to drive them home, but being single handed I just managed to cut those twelve free." "What are we waiting for," said Dudden, "Let's go and get those cattle." "I'll go with you, and show you the spot," volunteered Peter. All went quickly to the bridge, where Dudden jumped in, quickly followed by Hudden, who was equally greedy to get the big herd of cattle, and Peter Maguire went home with the biggest smile you have ever seen. It was probably eleven o'clock when I got home that night but I think the story was well worth losing some sleep for.

I looked forward to playing in the band and each year we played at the annual parades in Enniskillen, or the neighbouring towns and villages. Sometimes the band sounded better than others, and when things went well we were all very happy. In the early years of my time in the band, Desmond Lang, Hugh Buchanan, David Hassard, and myself made up the back row and played the 'F' flute. I always enjoyed the harmony created by the different sections as they played their parts. We had the drums out at the front, followed by the firsts playing the melody, then the seconds putting in an alto accompaniment and the F's doing the bass. All kept in time by the bass drummer. To name just a few, we played the marches, Galanthia, Kelly's Eye, Officer of the Day, and Oswald the Second in well balanced harmony.

Parades weren't always without incident or some good laughs. When we were standing in the field waiting to form up in the parade, Jack Thornton had a great habit of getting a piece of grass, coming up behind someone, and tickling the back of their neck with it. The reaction was sometimes funny when the person at the receiving end thought it was a wasp and started swiping away wildly with his hands to get rid of it, but sometimes he chose the wrong man to tickle and they would make a swing with their fist at him, or tell him to "grow up." Jack was most enthusiastic about anything he did, and loved to talk about silage making when he got his first forage harvester. Bertie Irvine said that one day, when they were both out with the band, they went along to have a cup of tea and Jack started to explain to Bertie how he cut his silage. Bertie said he went round and round his plate demonstrating, and only for he lifted his hand quickly he would have cut off his fingers when he was doing the back swath.

I remember Bobby Thornton getting us all lined up for a

cup of tea, and to speed things up he got a bag of sugar. Then as we went past he put the sugar in for us. The man in front of me said, "Two spoons please Bobby," Bobby obliged, not with a teaspoon, but with a large wooden cake mixing spoon which he had concealed behind his back. The two spoonfuls just about half filled his cup.

The band had quite a few characters in it, although I never saw myself as one. However, I recall one day as I was approaching the assembly point where a couple of the bands-men were having a chat and a laugh. I went over to hear what the laugh was about, and as I got nearer I heard one of them, who had a speech impediment saying, "Mar-mar-mar-malade, that's another big word." Sometimes the rows of players got out of line as we marched along. On one occasion as the band marched up Church Street in Enniskillen, a young lad, who was something of an nuisance at the best of times, somehow managed to step back onto the toes of the man behind, who immediately drew his foot and gave him a good resounding kick up the backside, which produced a loud "Yow!" and added, "Maybe that'll   teach you not to step back onto my toes."

A lot of the older members got past playing and retired from the band, which then reached a low ebb. I remember only Desmond Lang, Ollie Fawcett, and myself turning up for a band practice. But a recruitment campaign brought in new members and when I returned from Australia in 1976 the band had a well increased membership, and for the first time since the band was formed in 1895 included some girls. We kept up the practising and bought new uniforms in 1992, and then got a grant which helped with the purchase of new Silver flutes in 1996. Mullaghy Band was the first flute band in County Fermanagh to use them.

Farm Workers

Life changed for me after leaving school. There was the daily morning routine of milking the cows, feeding the pigs, feeding the young calves and leaving the full milk cans out to the road for collection. These were the chores Dad and I carried out while Mother prepared breakfast for the three of us. She of course, had a large flock of hens to attend to during the course of the day. Unlike a lot of farmers, my father believed in having a starting time and a finishing time. Farm life started with the milking of the cows about seven o'clock in the morning, and finished with the evening milking of the cows again at six p.m.

Down the years, my father always employed a man to help him on the farm, but now that I had finished with school this wasn't necessary. The last man he employed was John Hassard, who was with us for about eight years. My father only took on the extra help when the farm was busy, which meant John was with us from the beginning of March, until the end of October each year. John was a decent, easy-going type who lived near to the village of Bellanaleck, and cycled to our farm daily. A distance of about two and a half miles. John and I got on very well, but I did annoy him on at least one occasion. In the earlier days, when I came home from primary school, I was given the task of bringing out the afternoon tea to my father and John if they were working in the bog at turf or putting in the potato crop.

I remember my father had John employed with the horse and cart putting farmyard manure along the drills for the potatoes. I came home from school and arrived down into the field to see what John was doing. He had still some manure to empty so I stood watching, as John unloaded the cart from the back with a manure graip. He commanded the horse to walk on a little further as he followed along dropping graipfuls of manure into the drills. All was going nicely, but being a small boy and short of patience, I lifted some small clods of soil off the ground and threw them at the horse, which immediately started off down the drills. For the first time John lost his temper with me, and came running at me with the graip held high, and shouting at me for disturbing the horse. I took to my heels and ran off home. I told my mother John had shouted at me. Later on when John came up to the farmyard, he told the story correctly. By this time he had calmed down, and was laughing at how I had been afraid of him. Most Saturdays were spent in John's company, and were largely uneventful, but on one occasion he was trimming the hedges down the lane-way, when he said something which annoyed me. We were at the well on the turn of the lane near the house, where the cows came to drink in winter, and where Dad cooled the milk overnight in the summer. I told him that I was going to push him into the well. He said I wouldn't be able, and suggested that I take a run at him from across the lane. I went across the lane, but changed my mind, thinking if he went in the water I would get into trouble with my parents. I said I had changed my mind, and he said he would have side-stepped and let me run straight into the well. The mean rascal. The well was about three or four feet deep, so I wouldn't have drowned, he could have easily pulled me out.

When I was about nine years old, my father purchased his first tractor. I remember he went to see a second-hand one that was for sale, but decided a new one would be a better buy. The tractor was great, and I always enjoyed a Saturday when the tractor was in use. Drawing in the hay ricks was really fun. My father used a broad, low, flat bodied, wooden trailer, called a rick-shifter. It had a tipping mechanism which allowed the rick to be winched up the flat body. Two steel cables were unwound from the winding gear at the front and put around the base of the rick. These were hooked together and the cables were wound up with a handle, like a windlass, which wound the rick up unto the shifter. One day, my sister and I were sitting on the side of the empty rick-shifter, near to the front, going down to the meadow for another rick, and John was sitting at the tail, realising that the tipping mechanism wasn't locked, I whispered to Vera to move slowly towards the tail. Of course this shifted the centre of gravity, and without our counter balance, up went the front of the shifter, and down went John. Dad who was driving the tractor, heard the tail of the shifter scraping the ground and stopped, so that John could get on board again. Our house and farmyard were on a hill top, and my father had made a lane-way down to the lower land, as it was impossible to get up and down the hills in wet weather. At the meadow where the lane finished we took a sharp right-hand turn into the next field, and poor

John had a couple of mishaps here. He was sitting on the left side of the shifter, and I was on the back of the tractor as we went down the hill. John decided he would have a smoke on his pipe and was using both hands in the re-lighting process as we neared the turn at the meadow. I whispered to Dad, to not slow for the corner, and sure enough as we took the sharp right-hand bend, the centrifugal force sent John whizzing off into the field. I used to manage this trick on him about twice each year, but he always took it as good fun, even though he was at the receiving end. John was fond of a pull on his pipe but nearly set himself on fire a couple of times, as he drove in the cows for milking. Maybe a cow went the wrong way, and while he ran to turn her, John quickly pushed the pipe into his jacket pocket, and then forget about the lit pipe until he smelt the cloth smouldering. We used to laugh at these lapses.

It reminds me of an old fellow who was coming home from Enniskillen one Christmas Eve after having too much to drink. As he cycled past the Five Points cross-roads, one of the chaps standing there shouted at him, "Your coat's on fire," to which he replied, "And the same to you." (which was the usual thing to say if greeted by the words, "Happy Christmas.")

John called back to our house on a few occasions after he stopped working for us. On one occasion I remember him recalling how he had trouble with some of his teeth that had got a bit sharp, and were cutting into his tongue. He said he got a flat steel file, used for sharpening mowing machine blades, and levelled his teeth with it, and he had great comfort since. My father once pulled a tooth for him. He and John were drawing farmyard manure away with the tractor and trailer from the large pit that had accumulated over the winter, and were spreading it on the meadows where it provided the nutrients and organic matter for the production of a plentiful crop of grass. As they manually loaded the trailer with manure graips, John was complaining of a loose tooth in the front of his bottom jaw. After a while my father said, "Let's see where this tooth is." Seeing it was very loose, he took a pair of pliers out of the tractor tool box, and gripping John's tooth firmly, pulled it out with a quick jerk. John had comfort immediately and was delighted.

My father had a workman called Gilleece, who he said was the best workman he ever had. He was with us before John, and although I was quite small, I remember one happening which took place when some neighbours children came to our house one afternoon during the school holidays. We were all playing outside, and made our way around to the back of the hay-shed, where the wind had uprooted a fir tree in the small planting there. My father had trimmed the branches all the way along it, except for the last three feet at the top. I think he had intended to have it sawn up for timber at the local saw mill some time later, but hadn't got around to it. Albert said, "Come on and help me and we can put it up again." We all joined in, starting at the top, and went hand over hand along the twenty feet or so, until it was vertical again. The large root area dropping back into its original place. It was a reprieve in a sort of way for the tree, because it remained in place for years with it's few branches at the top until it was eventually removed to make way for a new silage pit. Then Mother called us in for tea, and Mary got into banter with Gilleece, who said, "My girl, I'll fix you yet before you go home." When we finished the tea and went outside again, Gilleece was waiting. He grabbed Mary, and carried her off under his arm, and tied her firmly to the windmill pole in the orchard at the back of the house, with the horse reins. So there was Mary completely helpless while we all laughed at her. Eventually we untied her, but I think she had learned not to tangle with Gilleece.

My father was not a man to tell many stories, but the exception was in the bog. When we went to the bog, which adjoined the farm, to cut the turf each spring, my father would tell of some past happenings. One of these involved a fellow called McFadden. He came from Glengavlin, which is an area of poor quality rocky land at the base of Cultiagh mountain in County Cavan. McFadden was hired by my grandfather at the hiring fair in Blacklion, to come and work for the summer on our farm. He proved to be an unhandy sort of man, which was immediately evident when my grandfather asked him to clean out the cow byre. McFadden filled the cow manure into the barrow, and made a charge for the door, but half time he collided with the door frame which was only about six inches wider than the barrow, and spilt the contents, only to have the job of refilling the barrow. As my father pointed out, had the 'clatty eejit' taken it slowly, he could have got through the door easily. Then when he arrived at the dunghill, he had another problem. The firm manure and straw mixture was built up a few feet high, and a nine inch wide plank was in place to wheel the barrow up to deposit each barrow-full on top. Of course our friend made a plunge at this also, and usually ran off the plank about halfway up, meaning he had to refill his load again. He would then sit down on the grassy bank and talk to himself saying, "Boys, but I'm hard wrought here." My father and his three brothers, who were young boys at this time, got great enjoyment watching the escapades of poor McFadden through the deep foliage of a nearby white-thorn hedge. Soon he learned that the young fellows of the area went along to the nearest cross-roads for a chat or maybe a game of football if they weren't too tired after the farmwork was done each evening. One evening, at the "Five points," someone asked McFadden how he was getting on at Montgomery's. He replied, "There's nothing but work, more work, go to bed, and rise and work." After a month he asked my grandfather for the money owing to him as he wanted to go home for the weekend to see his folks. He readily agreed, and as McFadden went away from the farmhouse, he thought he was a bit fat looking. He went along to his room and sure enough, McFadden was wearing his old work clothes under his better ones. My grandfather knew he was gone for good but did nothing to stop him.

Another farm labourer, my father recalled was a fellow called McGullion. He was very hard to get out of bed in the morning. After being called to get up a few times, my father and his three brothers would go into his room, pull off the bedclothes, and land him on the floor. He would protest loudly in a strong Leitrim accent, "Shore I foond ye rightly." However once he was mobile he managed to do the work all right, unlike McFadden. Come Sunday morning he would get a basin of hot water and take it out to the hay-shed, along with his shaving equipment, and clean himself up before going to Mass. With a mirror mounted on an upturned barrow he would commence to shave. This was the time for the mischief to start. One of my fathers brothers, who were just young boys at this time would get a long stick and poke the farm bull, which was tied up in a nearby shed. The bull would let out a deep 'booh' and lash out with his foot, taking thuds out of the corrugated iron. The boys would be bursting themselves to keep from laughing out loud as McGullion would shout, "Stand up out of that would ye," as he continued to carefully shave along his soapy jaw line with his large cut-throat razor, unaware of what was upsetting the bull.

I recall another story my father told of a farmer who was a bit miserly and when he employed someone he wanted to get a lot of work done for his money. He worked the farm along with his son but when it was time to go to the bog to cut the turf he employed a man to make up the team of three. One to cut, one to fill, and one to wheel. He told his son to take the fellow along to the bog and strip the sods off the bank ready to start cutting, and then he would come along a little later and he was to pretend to be very hard on his father. The son did as he was told and kept scolding away to the workman about the auld fellow lying about the house, instead of coming to the bog to help them. "I tell you what we'll do, we'll make the 'auld divvle' move today, when he does come. I'll cut as hard as I can, and you fill your best, and we'll keep him running with the barrows." When the father eventually appeared the son shouted at him as he approached. "Where do you think you were all morning, leaving us all the work to do here," He then ran up to the father and gave him a couple of kicks in the backside and said, "come on and get a move on." The workman thought this was terrible treatment altogether for the old man, but the old fellow was as strong as a horse and kept up the speed all day. By evening they had the poor workman exhausted.

About the turn of the last century when there was no such thing as a health service, a lot of unfortunate people became beggars. These people lived a precarious existence at the mercy and kindness of farmers, who would always give them a meal, when they called at the farms. Whether they were lazy, or unable to find work, or just refused to work, I don't know. But a fellow called Jemmy Meale was a regular caller at my grandfather's house. Jemmy enjoyed a good plateful of cabbage, bacon, and potatoes, finishing with a spoonful of salt, which he said was good for the wee boys. (killed the worms.) My father used to laugh as he recounted how Jemmy arrived for his dinner one day, and began telling them about a row he had had with his wife. Jemmy said. "Me and Elizabeth had a terrible row this morning,…. but I said nothing!" A stranger called one day asking for a slice of bread. My granny gave him a newly baked oat-cake biscuit with a generous coating of butter on it. After a little while he knocked on the door again, and handed her back the oat-cake, saying, "Thanks very much for the butter, and here's your wee bouard (board) back".

Derrygiff

The townland of Derrygiff lies about five miles south west of Enniskillen. It is unique to the best of my knowledge in that no other townland in Ireland has this name. Some townland names can be found at four or five locations, even in the same county. The name Derrygiff became known countrywide, when a murder was alleged to have been committed there in 1939. I tell the story of this in the chapter called, 'The man with three thumbs.'

My family settled in County Fermanagh at the townland of Carry, Innishmore, in 1618, during the plantation of Ulster. In 1728 my ancestor William Montgomery moved to Derrygiff. William was most likely a newly married man then, and needed to get a farm of his own. Deciding on Derrygiff may have been because the landlord of Derrygiff was Nicholas Archdale, the grandson of Hugh Montgomery of Derrybrusk, who was the original landlord of Carry Innishmore where William was reared.

On his marriage in 1724 to Angel, heiress to the Archdale estates, Nicholas changed his name from Montgomery to Archdale, and went to live in Castle Archdale. Although Nicholas was the landlord, and from a completely different family of Montgomerys, there was an earlier marriage between these two Montgomery families. Nicholas is descended from the Montgomerys of Braidstane, while our family is descended from the Montgomerys of Hessilhead, both from Ayrshire, Scotland.

This original tenant, William Montgomery rented the entire townland of Derrygiff, apart from forty acres, and presumably built the stone walled, thatched roofed, farmhouse. William sub-let most of this area except about twenty acres, which he farmed to supply his family with, meat, milk, and vegetables, etc. I believe in those days, ten acres was sufficient area for a family to live on. He probably had a good income from his sub-letting also. I am told that most of Fermanagh was covered with trees and bushes in those days, so presumably the men were employed clearing the land, digging drains, and planting hedges to divide the land into fields of a workable size, for farming by horse, donkey, or manual labour.

In the twenty first century, with cars, and sealed tarred roads everywhere, one has to draw on the imagination as to what those early ancestors had to deal with. While the homestead on the hilltop at Derrygiff is an idyllic location now, it was very isolated in 1728. The present lane from the main Enniskillen to Swanlinbar road to the farm did not exist until after 1830. The section of the main Enniskillen to Swanlinbar road which now runs past Derrygiff and the Fivepoints was made about then. Before that the road to Swanlinbar went straight from Mullaghy over Skea Hill to Arney, and on straight to Swanlinbar. This resulted in the route from our farm before 1830 being in a north-westerly direction, out across the fields and down Oakfield lane, to reach the old Enniskillen to Belcoo road, a journey of well over a mile. I suppose this sort of thing was common at that time, and not ever having a convenient and easily reached road meant you didn't miss it.

A generation later, William's son, Thomas, divided this property amongst three sons, William, Edward, and James. William being the eldest son acquired just twenty eight acres while his brothers, Edward and James, had sixty acres each. In trying to figure out this uneven divide a couple of reasons comes to mind. First, the descendants of William junior's line of Montgomerys were gifted at carpentry, and made their living from cart making. He may have had that gift too, therefore he didn't need much land, but the second reason could be that there may have been two more sons to be catered for at the time their father Thomas started dividing up the land. During genealogical research I discovered two other Montgomerys, who may well be brothers of William, Edward and James. But I have no documentary or confirmed proof of this. There is an age gap of fifteen years between William and Edward which possibly means other children were born in these years including girls. If there were five sons to inherit, instead of three and an even divide was intended, then William's portion was in order. Circumstances could have changed and these two sons may have emigrated, or left the area for some other reason, which is why we have no record of them. So the remaining land got split between the two youngest sons, making our farm sixty acres including some bog-land. Because the farm passed from father to son, the names of the sub-tenants were still used to identify some of the fields. There was

Bleakley's Field, Harry's Garden, Corrigan's Meadow, and Crawford's Brae. These people lived in small mud walled houses, and farmed their few acres. Back in those times, when the population of Ireland was over eight million people, very few lived in towns, so the entire country was dotted with these houses, which could only be described as hovels. As years went by, and times changed, these houses became disused due to migration, and the effect of the great famine of the eighteen forty's. Unlike a stone built house, mud walled houses were levelled out and disappeared quickly. I knew the location of four of them on our farm.

The land in this part of Fermanagh is mostly shallow soil resting on a bed of yellow or blue impervious clay and therefore becomes very wet and friable if it gets too much rain, which is often the case. This problem meant that cattle were housed for about five months of the year, and in turn required a lot of winter feed, such as hay or silage. Farm life was not easy, as cattle require continuous attention. I personally never liked cattle, and would have preferred an arable farm. In the end I decided to take my family to Australia where at least it would be warm and sunny. I later realised that my friends were in Ireland, so back we came realising sunshine wasn't everything. In fact it is much harder to endure continuous sunshine than the Irish rain.

I took a Canadian cousin to see the original homestead in the summer of 2003, and realised I had forgotten the view from the farmyard, that's to be had on a clear day. The green rolling hills of the surrounding countryside, stretching for miles in all directions with the man-made divisions of hedges and ditches giving a patchwork quilt appearance to the whole view, edged with the blue hue of the distant mountains, it really does make a beautiful landscape. Looking south you see Cultiagh mountain on the border of County Cavan, and looking north one can see Brougher mountain in County Tyrone. Even though the farmyard is only about two hundred feet above sea level, most other hills in the area do not have houses on their summit, apart from the neighbouring Nixon and Elliott properties. From this lofty summit I could look down on most of the neighbouring farms, and see them out working in their fields, or moving their cattle.

My father got married in 1937 and the next year he decided to improve the farmhouse. The old house, which was a typical farmhouse of the time, was a single storey building with white washed walls, thatched roof, and had two windows to the left of the front door and one to the right. The walls were made from sandstones which had been collected from the land, and were probably very plentiful as they were unearthed during the construction of drains and sheughs.

My father decided to make it into a two storey house with a slated roof. He got a few estimates and finally decided to employ Mr Alec Elliott to do the job. Alex decided that the family could live in one half while the other half was being built. So one half of the house was stripped of its roof and the walls repaired as necessary and the work of the second storey on top of the old stone walls was begun. Alex insisted the new work should be a mass concrete construction. This was a highly labour intensive job at that time, as all the concrete had to be mixed with shovels, and carried in buckets up to the top and poured into the cavity between the casing timber, to make the new walls.

My grandfather Mavitty suggested that his cousin, Alan Stephenson from Manorhamilton, be asked to help. Alan was a local handyman in the Manorhamilton area, and from the reports of my uncles and parents, was a great character. He kept them laughing at his jokes and sometimes had poor old Alex pulling his hair out with frustration, as he fooled around instead of being serious about the job in hand. My father said that he sometimes made up stories to tell. He said when Alan was telling a lie he had this mannerism of always putting up his hand, and pulling on his ear lobe. On one occasion when the kitchen chimney was finished, Alex was up on the roof and shouted down to make a fire in the hearth, to see if the chimney would draw. My father lit up a good turf fire, and when it was well alight Alan says, "Wait to you see this," and threw a cup of water into it. The result was a cloud of ash rising up the chimney. When Alex, who was still on the roof saw this he shouted down, " Boys, there's a powerful draw in that chimney, it's lifting the ashes off the hearth."

Eventually the second half of the house was completed, and it stood majestically on the hilltop, measuring fourteen feet to the eaves, and with two evenly spaced chimneys protruding from the ridge cap. The front wall which was about forty five feet long, now had three windows along the upper storey and one each side of the central front door on the ground floor. Alex made a mould which he used to create a nice design in the plaster work at the edge of the windows, he also cut the board along the eves into curved shapes giving it a more ornamental appearance. My father recalled later that during the renovation, a man called one day, and told him he was a very foolish man spending all his money on a house. He said a man near him had done a similar thing, and was dead within the year. To which my father replied, "I hope I get longer than that."

The grey plastered finish remained untouched until 1961 when my mother asked Johnny Megaw to come and paint it before my eldest sister Audrey got married. Johnny arrived one Monday morning on his bicycle about ten o'clock, and started the painting which lasted for about two weeks. But Johnny came later and later each day, eventually arriving one day at half past one in the afternoon. My father, who liked an early start, asked Johnny why he arrived so late, and Johnny said, "Well Willie, I sometimes meet people along the road and have a chat, and today I had a couple of chats, but isn't there plenty of time, sure tomorrow is not even broken on yet." One day Johnny was talking to my mother and said, "You know Mrs Montgomery, the devil is after me today." She replied, "I thought you were a religious man Johnny, the devil is never after me." "And why should he be, sure he knows he has you already," replied Johnny. On his last day at painting the outside of the house my mother asked Johnny if he would re-do the wood-grained doors in the entrance hall. These led off to the Drawing room, Dining room, and Living room. Johnny took a look and said, "Yes, I'll do those for you certainly." "When can you come Johnny," she asked. "I'll come tomorrow Mrs Montgomery," he replied. Two weeks later Johnny arrived, and was confronted by my mother who said quite sternly. "Johnny, I thought you were an honest man," Johnny interrupted before she could finish, "What's wrong with you now." She continued, "The last day you were here I asked you when could you grain my doors, and you clearly said, I'll do them tomorrow, Mrs Montgomery." Johnny replied, "Sure I didn't wait until tomorrow, didn't I come today." Mother just had to laugh. Johnny had purchased a nice new pair of white painter's overalls to do the work at our house, but when the painting was finished the overalls had an ample supply of all the colours he had used, splashed all over them, as had the concrete apron which ran along the street close by the walls of the house. My mother asked Johnny if the paint would come off the concrete, and was told, "Not at all, sure if it comes off the concrete what would be the point of putting it on the walls." Poor Johnny's life was cut short when he was one of eleven people killed in the Remembrance day bomb planted by the I.R.A. in Enniskillen on 8th November 1987.

My father took a sensible approach to farming and only devoted time and energy to jobs that would improve his income, or ease the workload. This meant the expense of machinery was justified if the work got done in half the time, and a fraction of the effort.

He always reckoned that it was impossible to have too good a cow, figuring that a similar amount of feed and grazing area would be used by a cow giving six gallons of milk a day as on one giving three, but the profit margin would be greater. Looking back now his ideas were correct, and proved successful, but there was also a much better profit margin in farming in those days.

My father never spoke much about himself, but he did reveal that as a young boy he used to climb up onto the turf-house roof and run along the ridge cap in his bare feet. I would have got a sharp reprimand from him if I had ever attempted a similar exploit when I was young.

As a young man my father enjoyed game shooting, and used to invite some of the shopkeepers he traded with in town out to the farm to shoot pheasants when the shooting season started each October. Our farm joined up with a large expanse of bog so they had a good area to cover on these shoots. Another friend of his was an old man who had only one leg, and walked with the aid of crutches. But he enjoyed shooting rabbits which were very plentiful and something of an nuisance in the country side. He and my father used to go shooting. My father said he was a great shot. When a rabbit appeared he could prop his crutch, put up the gun, and still hit the rabbit. My mother told me this old man offered my father one of his daughters for a wife, but he obviously declined the offer. She told me his words were, "Be hanged to my buttons, Billy, but I'll give you the pick of the three of them."

George

Farming in Fermanagh in the late fifties and early sixties was still hard work, even though mechanisation had begun with the invention of the tractor years earlier. This was rapidly propelled and advanced by the compulsory tillage of the war years. Most farmers in our area of Fermanagh still used a horse for the main farm tasks. My father had purchased his first Ferguson TE20 tractor in 1951, and gradually acquired all the relevant implements for use with the tractor, to ease the burden of farming life. It was into these conditions that I found myself on leaving school in the mid-fifties. Although the main jobs such as ploughing, mowing, and potato digging were mechanised, it was still a manual job to trim the hedges all round the farm with a slash-hook. I used to lose patience with this task, and couldn't wait to have it finished.

While trimming the hedges along some of the lower meadows one day, our neighbour George, came over to chat to my father. George was a character of the area in my opinion. He always wore a cap, and having a bad knee he had difficulty walking, so he usually went around in a pony and cart, which had a pair of mowing machine wheels instead of the normal cart-wheels. The bore in the wheels was larger than the cart axle and allowed the wheels to wobble about from side to side as it went along, but had the necessary desired effect of dropping the back of the cart down very low, so he could get in and out of it easily. George started each sentence in a strong loud voice and gradually faded down to little more than a whisper. I found this very amusing as I listened to him recalling events to my father. He would start by saying, "Wait till I tell you a story Ma'gomery," at full volume, and then continue in diminishing tone, "You know we had twenty young turkeys being reared for the Christmas market, and one night we forgot to shut them in the house. Well wouldn't that be the night that a fox should come along. Next morning, I was heading out with the milk to the road when I twigged the feathers scattered along the field. I hadn't time to do anything then, but when I came home I went to investigate. What do you think Billy, if he hadn't killed them all but one." "That was an awful slaughter," interjected my father. "Aye! it was," responded George, "but wait 'till I tell you a better story, didn't he come back one day the next week in full daylight, and took the last one too! Did ever you hear the like of it?" continuing he said. "Fred Trotter was over in our house one night. We had a great chat, I hadn't been talking to him for a long time. You know what he was telling me Ma'gomery? He said that if you opened a gap into some man's field, and continued to use it, then after seven years you could claim it as your own. Sure that couldn't be right, for I was thinking that all you had to do was keep opening gaps, and in no time at all, sure wouldn't you own the half of the country." "Aye" responded my father, with a smile. George continued, "I was out for the empty milk cans at the road one day when Joe Thompson came along on the bike. He stopped for a chat, and in no time at all he was asking me how many cows I had milking, was I rearing any calves, had I any pigs now. You know what I said to him Billy, "I say Thompson, when did you get the job of lifting the census!" Then changing to a more domestic topic he asked, "Tell me Willie, what do you think of that cooker you have up there?" We find it a good job, and no smoke in the kitchen," replied my father. "I know you have it a long time now, and my woman thought we should get one. It was delivered one day and the young lassie couldn't wait to try a few scones in it. She made them up and put them in the oven to bake, well, we were ready for bed and they still weren't cooked, and what do you think but they weren't even done when we got up the next morning. I was sorry I had ever bought it, sitting there with a drip to your nose, I'm telling you thon's a 'cowl' looking boy." "That's funny," said my father, "Ours puts up a great heat." "Aye, well," said George, "We found out the secret afterwards........ you need to keep a good fire going in it."

George pranced around on the soft lush grass as he spoke, and I noticed that by now he had an area of at least a metre square all blackened by his continuous moving to and fro. Do you ever have any trouble with dogs, Willie? he asked, "We have trouble with them barking at night sometimes, and we have a few strays coming about from time to time, but they really don't give us that much trouble." my father responded, "Well that's not so bad I suppose," said George," but you know what I'm going to tell you, Willie, we were just tortured all last spring. You see I used to make up a pot of stirrabout (meal and water, boiled) for the calves, and leave it outside the door to have it cooled for morning. Been doing it for years and no bother at all, until this blaggard of a dog started coming during the night and would have the half of it eaten when we got up in the morning. I tried putting the lid on, but sure he knocked it off, and I even tried putting a brick on the lid, still no good. Then one day I thought why not shoot him! I thought there's no way that I'm going to sit up half the night waiting for him to come, and maybe not get him close enough to shoot anyway. So an idea came to me, why not drive a couple of pieces of timber into the ground, tie the gun firmly to them and connect a string across from the trigger to the pot lid, and then when 'Mr Thief' comes for his midnight feast, and knocks off the lid he would shoot himself. I got all set up and went off to my bed, and next morning not a thing was touched. I thought this is a very smart dog we're dealing with here. The next night I set it all up again, and about four o'clock in the morning – BANG. I got up and went out and there was the 'boyo' lying dead. That finished the eating of the calves feed! There was a man telling me that I shouldn't have shot the dog, but sure the way I looked at it was, he was vermin, the same as a rat, or a fox."

George got the mains water connected when the water main was installed along the road, as did all the other farmers in the area. He told a man one day, how handy it was, and that the water went out of the 'jaw-box' just as handy as it came in, and no need to heel it over or anything. Much delight was expressed by the local community in the late nineteen fifties when the mains water supply came. It did away with all that water carrying from wells, and springs. In fact, spring wells were scarce in the local area as a whole. We lived on a hill and had a spring well down at the bottom of the hill near the bog, on what we referred to as the back of the land. It had been divined by my grandfather Mavitty, who was much in demand for his divining skills. He had found water for people all around the local area and as far away as Manorhamilton. He used a forked stick of hazel and holding the ends firmly in his hands, he would walk along slowly until the point of the stick would twist down suddenly as he crossed over the run, which could be twenty feet deep. Sometimes water could be found seeping to the surface, in which case it was certain there was a reasonable well there, as there may have been a sand or gravel bed at that spot and water would accumulate naturally, being held there by the surrounding impervious clay. This type of underground water trap usually dried up in very dry spells but was okay for most of the year. We had one of these shallow spring wells down in a meadow at the front side of the farm. It was cleaned out a couple of times a year and used exclusively for drinking water in the house for generations, until my father had the well at the back, which was over twenty feet deep, built all round with bricks, a pipeline laid, and an engine and pump installed in a little house nearby to pump the water up to the house, a distance of about five hundred yards. This well never went dry, but was abandoned when the mains was installed.

During the years we were using the pumped water from the back well, our neighbours, the Elliotts used to draw water from our front well. The Elliotts had a large family of four boys, and four girls, and we used to help each other out at hay-making, potato planting, harvesting, and with the turf cutting and drawing them home when dried.

The front well has a story that only came to my attention while chatting to my Aunt Eileen one day. Her aunt, Elizabeth, who was the eldest girl in a family of twelve children, eight boys and four girls, had the task of carrying a couple of buckets of water from the well each day, and as the years rolled on and she became an attractive young woman. A young man who lived on the neighbouring farm took a fancy to her. Unfortunately her parents disapproved of the match, because she was a farmer's daughter and he was only a herd's son. The romance went on in secret for a time, eventually they realised her parents weren't going to change their mind, so what were they to do. A lot of people were emigrating to Canada at that time, and they thought that was what they should do too. So one morning, Elizabeth put on her best dress and her everyday one on top of it, took whatever personal belongings and money she had and went to the well with her buckets as usual. Her anxious boyfriend was there waiting for her with all the arrangements made, and off they went. After a considerable time her mother said. "Elizabeth is taking a long time at the well this morning, I hope she hasn't fallen in." They went down to the well and found the two buckets sitting there with a note attached to one of them. It said to not worry about her as she had gone to Canada with her boyfriend. It was quite sad for her family as they missed her very much and I'm sure she missed them too, but they married and lived happily in Canada, but never came back to Ireland, although some of their children did in later years.

The Young Farmers

As a teenager, I led a very restricted life, compared to life now at the start of the twenty first century. I had to always ask my parent's permission before going to a neighbour's house, or to some function at any of the local halls, and say what time I would be home. I was already a member of Mullaghy Flute band, and then I joined the 'Bellanaleck Young Farmers Club,' when it started in our area. The young farmers club was a very social place, and the fun was mighty at times. We were supposed to learn how to become better farmers, better countrymen, and better citizens. But with half the members being girls, and the age group between twelve and twenty-five, a lot of time was spent trying to woo the girls. Before Christmas, each year we had an excuse for a party, and usually invited our neighbouring club, 'Lisbellaw,' to join with us. I experienced my first real kiss at one of these. We played 'Down on the carpet,' The rhyme finishes with, Georgie, Porgie, kiss and run. So you got the chance to kiss your partner. Looking back now, I think the young farmers clubs were a great thing. It took a lot of shy and timid young lads, like myself, out of their shell and got them mixing with a group of other young people, which helped to develop social skills that previous generations didn't have. Our parents thought it was a complete waste of time and couldn't see it helping at all. We did learn how to judge cattle, how to make a speech, and how to conduct a business meeting. So it wasn't a complete waste. We were getting near the time of year when the public speaking competitions were taking place, so the headmaster from Enniskillen High School was invited out to give us some speech training. Although he spoke to us for an hour, the only thing that I remember him saying, was to, "Stand up! Speak up! and Shut up!"

We had many a good night's fun travelling to other clubs for quizzes, and parties too. On one occasion, we were coming home from Clogher in Ivan Loane's land rover, when Ivan felt the steering pulling hard to the left as we came into Brookeborough. A front wheel had got punctured. Luckily he had a spare, but on the dark unlit road it was going to be hard to get it changed. Then I had an idea. I had a small mirror in my pocket, and suggested we reflect some light from the head-lamps of the land rover onto the wheel. It worked a treat, giving enough light to get the wheel nuts off and on again. I still remember Ivan asking me to shine that torch over here a minute. We all laughed. We used to sing songs to pass the time while we journeyed to the more distant places. One that Ivan taught us went like this: Lloyd George knew my father, my father knew Lloyd George. After we repeated that bit three or four times, we asked him if that was all of it. "Oh no! there's another verse, it goes like this; My father knew Lloyd George, Lloyd George knew my father."

We were having a party in the small Parochial Hall at

Bellanaleck one night, and Cathal McConnell, the well known traditional flute player came to provide some music and entertainment for us. Bellanaleck was one of the first small villages in Fermanagh to have street lighting, and a lot of people thought it wasteful when there were only a few houses there at that time. Cathal made good use of the controversy by singing a song for us called, 'Milking the Cows by the Bellanaleck Lights.' The hall was very small and some of the Lisbellaw lads were running around outside. John Riley hopped up on a concrete milk stand, which was made on the roadside by George Cathcart for putting cans of skim milk on. These were tipped over into a trough on the other side of the wall to feed his pigs. Of course the dim streetlights showed a white surface on both sides of the wall, which John thought was concrete also, and jumped over, only to sink to his hips in the smelly buttermilk. Of course a few of the lads thought it would be a great idea to bring him into the hall, all wet and stinking with the buttermilk, but he couldn't be found. He had made his way down to Cathcart's hayshed. One of his friends drove a car down and stopped, then swung open a door. John shot out of the shed, got quickly into the car, and away they sped, while we all stood watching on the road at the hall about one hundred yards away. I still remember Jim Rooney remarking, "This has been the highlight of the evening." Poor John was known as 'Buttermilk Riley' for a good while after that.

Preparations for cattle judging competitions were usually in the springtime. We went around the farms of different club member's for practice sessions. Four milk cows, four dry cows, or four maiden heifers were selected by the farmer and the training judge, to be placed in order. A.B.C.D. A good tip was to select what you thought was the very best one, and then the worst one. Then if you had the middle two wrong it wasn't a big mistake. After placing the animals, each person had to go in front of the judge, and say why they had placed the four animals in that particular order. Most times the animals were so well matched that there was hardly any difference in them. So if you were lucky enough to have the same judge as on another occasion, you had half the battle over. We found that one judge would look mainly for good body confirmation, while another one might prefer good udder attachment and teat placing.

Victor Nixon and I were coming home in Victor's car one evening from a cattle-judging practice when we saw a car in Victor's dad's field, on the corner near our lane. We stopped the car off the road and went to investigate the accident. We found that four lads from Cavan were heading to Enniskillen Town hall to hear Ruby Murray, who was a big recording star at that time. They had misjudged the corner, gone over the hedge, and tumbled their small mini car. The only visible damage we could see was the front windscreen had sprung out under the impact, and was lying intact on the field, while the car had finished up, back on it's wheels a little further away. Victor went up to his house and brought down the tractor, and some baler twine. We soon had the windscreen back in place, tied in firmly with the string to the windscreen wiper bases and a little drain hole in the roof guttering on the mini. They were so pleased when we towed them back unto the road. The engine started again okay and one lad slipped me ten pounds and said, "Split that with your friend, you have done a good job for us tonight." They didn't get to hear Ruby after all, and had to return back home feeling a bit shocked by their experience.

The highlight of the Y.F.C. year was the annual excursion to the Isle of Man, Scotland, or some of the Scottish Isles. I went on two of these excursions. The first time I went, it was on the encouragement of my neighbour David Hassard. I set my alarm, and got up at two o'clock in the morning, had a small breakfast, and cycled down to David's house. He and his sister Daisy had arranged for Daisy's friend, Carol Elliott to call for us with her car, and then pick up Jim Rooney at his house. The five of us drove over to Fivemiletown, where we joined up with some of the County Tyrone clubs, who had hired a bus to take us all to the cross channel ferry at Belfast Harbour. We arrived in Belfast around seven o'clock, and set sail at eight o'clock for Douglas on the Isle of Man. It was my first time on a ferry, and although it's a comparatively small vessel by ocean going liner standards, I thought it was huge. David and I soon left the comfortable lounge area and went exploring the rest of the ship. By the time we had moored up at Douglas at one o'clock we had been all over the different decks and felt confident that we had seen the entire boat. All eighteen hundred on board were eager to get off as quickly as they could and the weight of everybody crushing for the gang-plank caused the ferry to list to that side quite considerably, but we all managed to disembark safely.

The trip to Douglas was just for one day, but what a day. We took the horse drawn tram along the promenade; we had a good meal in a restaurant, and even did a trip on the electric train out to the little town of Laxey, to see the big wheel there. By afternoon I was feeling the loss of my sleep, and the steady throb of the train as we chugged along in the open sided carriages, didn't help matters. But I managed to stay awake, and enjoyed the trip. Six o'clock arrived all to soon, and time to go on board the ferry again. We made our way to the harbour, and up the gang-plank onto the ferry. On the deck above us, as we made our way up, were a bunch of lads who had spent most of their time in the bar drinking beer on the outward trip, but now they were singing, 'Down by the river side,' in lovely harmony. One big tall fellow with a long neck was putting in a lovely deep bass, which went, 'Down by, down by.' I wondered afterwards if they had gone on shore at all, but had maybe spent the day on board sleeping off the effects of their morning's drinking. Back on board some slept, some sang, and some just chatted in groups and it seemed a shorter journey home. We arrived in Belfast again about eleven thirty and then continued the return bus and car journey home to Fermanagh. I finally got to bed about three thirty in the morning, feeling very sleepy, after all I had missed a full nights sleep.

I was called about eight o'clock next morning, and told to hurry up and have my breakfast. My father had the milking done already, and was anxious to get some silage cut. It was the month of June and without my help he hadn't been able to get much done the day before. So it was action stations, and full speed ahead. I got the mower onto the tractor and drove away down to the bottom meadows to cut the grass. Oh Boy!, the lack of sleep started to get to me, as I drove round and round the field, with the engine throbbing away steadily, and the mower blade clicking, as it shuttled back and forth in a steady rhythm. Looking back now I see the danger I was in. Tractors did not have safety cabs then, and being so sleepy I could well have fallen off the tractor, which would most likely have been fatal, as I would hardly have missed both the tractor rear wheels and the mower. My only hope came with the square corners. Because it was a small field, the corners soon became square which meant that I had to lift the blade, and reverse back at each corner, turning the tractor around ninety degrees, to line with the next side of the field. Doing this at each corner broke the monotony, and kept me alert. I managed to complete the job safely, and slept well that night. My father's attitude was, if you are able to go gallivanting off for a day, then you should be able to work the next one.

Harvest

I first drove the farm tractor when I was ten years old. It was a petrol-engined Ferguson TE20, which was a light handy machine, capable of doing most of the farm work. It was used very little in the winter time, except when potatoes were needed at the farmyard. Potatoes were stored in long triangular shaped pits in the field where they were harvested. They were first covered with a thatch of straw, or more usually rushes, and then covered all over with a six to nine inch covering of soil to keep out rain, frost, and light. (potatoes go green and poisonous if exposed to daylight.) Being about nine years old at this time, my job was to hold the large jute bags open, while my father filled them up using a potato graip. The potato graip had round knobs on the ends of the prongs, so it didn't stick into the potatoes. We usually brought home about half a ton at a time, which kept the pigs fed for a few weeks.

The tractor came into more use as the year went on. The first job was to spread the artificial manure on the grassland as soon as growth had started, so that the cattle which were housed all winter could be let out onto the fresh pasture again. Then, as the days got longer, and the arable land dried out, it was time to plough and cultivate the ground for the crops of potatoes and oats. As soon as the crops were in, the next job was the cutting of the turf, normally about the first week of May. We were fortunate to have the bog included into our farm. Some farmers whose land did not include bog had to travel miles to cut their turf. Their plots were located in large areas of bog belonging to the landlords and usually administered by trustees. Cutting the turf was a hard back-breaking job in my experience.

The first thing was to mark out the area for cutting with a well tensioned line of string, usually a section of the bank four feet wide and about twenty yards long. Then using a sharp spade, the bog was marked along the line. Next it had to be stripped down about six inches to remove the heather and bog cotton roots. This was dug off in large sods from the top with the spade and thrown down into last years bog hole, before getting at the usable peat. Only then could the actual cutting begin. Three men were employed. One used a special turf-cutting spade with a wing on it which made a right angled cut and separated each turf, as he cut the turf out in rows. The second man lifted three or four of the freshly shaped turf at a time and placed them on a special flat turf barrow, usually putting on two rows wide and two rows high, with one row on top down the centre, known as a binder. The third man then wheeled the loaded barrow out across the bog and dumped each barrow-full, making rows which were later spread out flat to dry after they had firmed up a little. Two barrows were used, so that one was being filled when the other one was being emptied, making the work continuous. The bank of turf was usually cut out in six floors, each floor being eight or nine inches deep. The complete block of four feet wide and twenty yards long and about five feet deep being removed in one day. I was young and fit, and working in the bog gave me a great appetite, so I was always delighted when my mother blew the whistle indicating that the midday dinner was ready for us. The new seasons cabbage were usually big enough to eat at this time of the year, and we all enjoyed the bacon, cabbage and potato dinner, followed by custard and jelly. Mother usually brought out afternoon tea to us in the bog, which gave us a short break in the work about three o'clock. We finished at six, and then went home and eat a dish of rice pudding which mother had waiting for us, before doing the evening milking.

The turf cutting lasted about four or five days. This produced enough turf to keep the fire going for the whole year, If the weather was good, each barrow-full of turf was spread out after a week or two, to dry. When dry, they shrunk to about half their original size, and were then built into neat piles, called clamps, usually about three feet long, one foot wide, and about two feet high, tapering in to just one turf along the top row. These were built in neat rows, and left to season and dry out completely, before being drawn home to the turf shed where they were stored, and used for burning in the fire in the dwelling house. Working at turf was a slow back-breaking job, but apart from the labour, it was a cheap source of fuel. I heard of a man who called to visit my grandfather one time and the talk came around to winning the turf. My grandfather said he had his all won and in the turf-shed. The visitor remarked. "You'll be lucky if you don't have to cut them again." He was indicating that they couldn't possibly have been fully dried when he put them in the shed, and would stick together into a large block.

Hay making came next on the agricultural calendar, and in the early fifties my father usually started this task in early June. If the weather was good the grass was cut and left to wilt a day or two, then the swaths were turned over to allow wilting of the other side. When the hay felt dry, and crackled when crunched up, it was considered dry enough to be gathered up and built into ricks. These were left in the meadows to season for two or three weeks before being taken home and stacked in the hay-shed. This was the main winter diet for generations, and provided the winter fodder for the horses, cows, and calves before silage making became popular in the nineteen fifties and sixties. In 1955 my father built our first silage pit and this meant we were less dependant on good weather, as silage could be made in showery weather, although dry days were best for it too.

We always tried to have the turf home before the hay-making started but the farmer can't decide when to do a job. It always depended on the weather being suitable. Even though the war was over about seven years, and compulsory tillage no longer in force, the farmers still grew a lot of potatoes, turnips, oats, and barley. During the drawing home of the oats, I got to drive the tractor for the first time. I was absolutely thrilled. This was just the greatest thing for me to get doing. The oats, or corn as it was commonly called, was cut when ripe, and tied into sheaves, which were then gathered into stooks of about ten sheaves, to dry and season for a few weeks, before being drawn home to the farmyard where they were built into round stacks. It was during the drawing home of the stooks that my father told me to drive the tractor on the few yards from one stook to the next one, while he and John loaded the trailer. I was delighted with my job and having watched my father carefully as he drove the tractor. I knew what to do without any instruction, It saved my father having to get up and down off the tractor all the time as the trailer had to be moved along from stook to stook.

Later on in the season, word spread around the neighbourhood that a thresher was in the district. Arrangements were then made with the contractor as to when he could thresh our corn. It was amazing how these big wooden threshers, usually on four rubber tyred wheels, and pulled along by a large tractor, would cross from farm to farm. Not by the road and lanes, but usually a gap was made in the boundary hedge, and straight onto the next farm. A man called James Brown came that year, he came through from the Elliott's farm, and proceeded up the hill to our house. He steered the old T.V.O. Fordson Major tractor, with the engine giving the occasional misfire, carefully round into the haggard. He had an oily looking cap slightly askew on his head, and was puffing contentedly on his crooked-shanked pipe, which hung from the corner of his mouth. Steadily, he manoeuvred the thresher into a suitable position close to the hay-shed and the corn stacks. He then unhooked the tractor and reversed it back to the other side of the tresher, lining up the flat pulley on the side of his tractor with the large one on the thresher. Next the long flat belt was fitted over the pulleys, and the tractor moved back a little further to tension the belt, all was now ready to go. The day the thresher came was a notable event on the annual farming calendar. My father had gathered up a group of neighbours and friends to help with the threshing. There were two men pitching up the sheaves from the stacks onto the thrasher, two men up on top of the thrasher cutting open the sheaves and feeding them down into the flailing drum, two men carrying the straw away from the front and building it up in the hay-shed, and a man attending the bags of grain as they were filled up at the back. My job was to keep our terrier dog in a good position to catch any rats or mice as they tried to escape from the stacks. There were some, and we managed to catch several of them. The trouble was that the dog could only catch one at a time, and if a few ran out simultaneously some escaped. A cat on the other hand was useless because it would go off and eat each mouse as soon as it caught it, letting all the others escape. The threshing day didn't go unnoticed in the house as it gave my mother a lot of extra work preparing dinner and tea for everybody, as was the custom.

I heard a story one time that was told by John Brodison, who was well known for the telling of tall tales. John said that he was helping one day at a threshing, and the farmer told one of the men to take the tying ropes and thatch off the corn stacks, and have them ready for pitching onto the thresher when it arrived. The man put a ladder up against one of the stack and climbed up to the top to start, when he suddenly disappeared from view. John was told to see where he had gone and climbed up the ladder. On getting to the top he looked down through the hole. It was literally hiving with rats. They had eaten the entire centre out of the stack, and only a few bones were left of the poor fellow that had fallen in a few minutes earlier.

The day of the threshing was quite a social event, and

usually about half an hour or so would be spent after the dinner was eaten, relaxing and telling the occasional story. I remember a story told about a man who lived close by who had a speech impediment. Although the poor fellow couldn't help it, every one had to laugh. It seems that Willie was driving some bullocks to the fair in Enniskillen one day when someone passed by in a car travelling at high speed. The bullocks had spent their entire life grazing the hills on Willie's farm, and had never been on the road before, so when the car passed by, they immediately took fright, some of them jumping through the hedge into a field. Now cattle are strange in that they will go through a small hole in a hedge if frightened, but flatly refuse to return through the same hole. Any one used to working with cattle knows this, and would drive them along until a suitable gate or gap was found, but not Willie. He was determined that he would put them back out onto the road by the same hole as they had made getting in. So Willie was running the cattle up and down past the hole in the hedge, shouting. "A-jumpy-in, a-jumpy-out."

Willie was playing football with the local lads at the 'Five points' one evening when his neighbour accidentally kicked him on the shin with his heavy hob-nailed boot. He immediately took Willie off home thinking he had broken Willie's ankle. On arriving at the house Willie's mother asked, "Do you know anything about this Freddy"? "Naw!" said Freddy, and him being the culprit who had done it.

Freddy loved to sing and entertained on many an occasion at Gransha Hall. He used to sing a song called, 'Standing at the corner of the street,' and another one called 'Four and nine.' Freddy lived on a small farm with his sister Lizzie, neither of them married, but a neighbour man took a liking to Lizzie, and used to visit regularly in their house. Lizzie would laugh and joke with him, and then after he had gone home, she would say, "The clatty auld eejit, shur I hate the sight o'him." Someone said that Lizzie had a baking board on which she made her soda bread, but she never bothered to clean it, and over the years there was a build up of dough greatly reducing her working area. Finally she was only able to make a bun on it. It was said that Lizzie was making bread one day and the cat kept jumping up onto the table where she was mixing up the ingredients. Lizzie would knock her down with a swipe of her hand, and continue on with her baking. I told this to my friend Bill one day, and he replied with a smile, "There must have been a mousey smell off the flour, Bob."

The next big job was the digging of the potatoes. This took place in the month of October and was another milestone of the farming year. Our farm had an area of peaty soil on the low meadows, which lay between the hills and the bog where the turf was cut. This ground had once been virgin bog-land, and after hundreds of years of cutting and removing the turf, the remaining rich black soil was ideal for producing root crops. Turf rather than coal was used by everyone in the country areas of Ireland as a fuel for heating their houses. It was also cheaper and locally available. When I was a boy, my father used to grow about an acre of turnips, some mangolds, and usually three acres of potatoes. All these crops were used to feed the cattle, pigs, and poultry on the farm. The potatoes were planted in drills, the soil was set up in a raised v-shape made with the horse and a special drill plough, and then dug out at harvest time with spades. The arrival of the tractor greatly eased this heavy workload, especially the potato digging. Instead of my father and John spending weeks with the spade, it now only took a matter of minutes to whizz out each drill of potatoes with the tractor and potato digger. Our neighbours, the Elliott's, also planted a lot of potatoes, so it made sense to combine our efforts. They came to help us gather our potatoes, and we went to help them with theirs. This worked out well for all, and with seven or eight gathering the potatoes, the entire drill was soon picked up. We each had our own section of only a few yards to collect, and then it was time to dig out another drill. Sometimes, two of us boys would be filling into the same bucket, and for a bit of mischief, one would quickly pull the bucket away, just as the other had thrown his handful of potatoes. Of course these missed the bucket, and had to be collected again. It was taken in good part as long as it only happened occasionally, and never led to bad humour, as the nonsense was shared.

The Elliotts had a large family of four boys, and four girls. John, the eldest, was a little older than me, and we all went to the same school, but never got to know each other well, until John bought himself an old car when he was eighteen. I had done my driving test in my father's car when I was seventeen, so as a holder of a full licence I was allowed to accompany a learner driver. John needed plenty of practice so he asked me to accompany him in his car as he practised his driving around the roads of Fermanagh. I got a shock when I saw his car. He had told me it was old, but it was ancient. An Austin ten about thirty years old with the dividing pillar between the front and back door rusted through at the roof. Each time John closed his door, he had to prop the pillar with his elbow to keep it firm while he slammed the door closed. The headlights gave off a very poor beam, and on my first trip out in this ancient machine I felt anything but confident, and imagined us grinding to a halt on some country road and having to walk home. We churned along at about twenty miles an hour, and decided to do a short journey by way of the Five Points, Arney, Bellanaleck, turn towards Enniskillen, and back home by way of Riley's cross. We had just passed the village of Arney when the shuddering and rattling changed to a definite thumping underneath the car. It was time to stop. John had a small torch with him, and taking a quick look under the car we soon discovered what was causing all the noise. Of the four bolts securing the drive-shaft joint, all but one had sheared or broken, and the shaft, hanging on by one corner, was hitting the car floor each time it turned. We needed at least one bolt and a couple of spanners to fix it temporary, and resume our journey. Luckily John had an adjustable spanner and a set of pliers, so we started looking around the car to see if we could find a suitable bolt. I noticed that the radiator was bolted in, and thought we could remove one of them, and use it for our repair. We managed to undo the rusty bolt, and crawled underneath the car and reconnected the drive shaft. It was time to see if our repair would hold, and sure enough we were able to continue. The car was running much smoother than before, as the loose shaft had been causing a lot of vibration. On our next trip out we went to John Ross who had a small workshop at Letterbreen and he replaced all four bolts in the drive shaft. He also rewired one of the headlights to a separate switch on the dashboard. It so greatly improved the lighting that John was considering if he should have the entire wiring replaced. John Ross told him to replace the entire car instead. The following week John took his advice and traded the old Austin in for a nice second hand Morris Minor. He was now driving in luxury, and quickly became confident enough to do his driving test, which he passed with flying colours.

John's younger brother came seeking my help one day. He was working in a factory in Enniskillen, and as they worked shifts, it soon came his turn to do the night shift. He found he could do what he liked during the day, and didn't bother to sleep in the daytime. He managed two days, and then on his return home from work on the third morning he fell asleep as he was driving in the lane to his house. The car ran off the side of the high lane and slid down the bank into a deep drain, coming to a halt on its side. The final bump wakened him, and because he had been going very slow little damage was done to either the car or himself. The problem then was how to get the car back onto the lane. He thought I could use the tractor to pull him back up onto the lane, but on a close examination, I concluded that I would damage the car and it may tumble over unto its roof when I tried to move it. The only answer was to get a crane to lift it up straight out of the drain. He took my advice and got a local breakdown recovery man to lift the car safely back onto the lane. After this experience he also took his proper sleep during the daytime when working night shifts, so two lessons were learned that day.

Before he started working in the factory he had been working at home on the family farm, and taking the advice of a neighbour, he had purchased a young sow in the hope of making some money rearing pigs. He got up one morning and went to feed the sow, only to find she had broken the door, and was nowhere to be found. He set off to look for the sow and a helpful neighbour told him that Ireland was an island and he would find her some place. He eventually found her underneath his father's car. She had crawled in underneath the car and was firmly wedged in the small six-inch space. To pull her out might damage the car, and finally someone said, why not jack up the car. He got the sow back into her house and later sold her back again to his neighbour. That was the end of the pig farming enterprise, but he went on to do factory work, and eventually became the owner of a licensed restaurant.

Sammie

It's a great pity that all these old characters are no longer with us, but maybe young folk today see us older ones as the characters. Sammie Higgins was one of these characters. Sammie was a man of medium build and height, with a good crop of frizzy, gingery / brown hair. Sammie's claim to fame lay in his great strength. He said he was constructed from high carbon steel. He wrote to one of the national newspapers to see if they would write his life story, profiling all the exploits, escapades, and feats of strength that he had done in his lifetime. They asked him for a draft of his story, but Sammie refused to disclose any information until he got paid. The letters went back and forth for years, and then when he was about eighty years old, he eventually asked David Nixon, a local schoolmaster, to come over to the house one evening. David arrived with his neighbour Desmond. Sammie came straight to the point, "Master Nixon, you are a well educated, intelligent man and I would like you to write my life story." David readily agreed and asked him for the details, but Sammie said, "I need the money first before I divulge a word, otherwise I'll take it all to the grave with me." "How can I write your story if you won't tell me what it is," said David, whereupon Sammie said,

"Come here and I'll show you." They went outside to where there was a large pile of old iron bars. Sammie bent down and lifted up about one hundred kilos of them in his arms. "Now do you see what I'm capable of, and I was even better when I was younger, and if you want further proof, then write to this man in Canada," he exclaimed, pulling Clements Hanna's address out of his pocket, "He will tell you what I'm capable of." Of course the story was never written because Sammie still refused to tell it.

Sammie had only a small farm and took part time employment with local farmers. Clements Hanna was a progressive farmer in the area before he decided to emigrate to Canada. He had employed Sammie to help him remove some hedges, so he could enlarge his fields, and make them easier to manage with the larger tractor-powered machines that were starting to come on the market. One of the hedgerows had a lot of large ash trees growing along it. These had been cut down and sawn up for firewood, while the lighter branches were strewn along the ground. Clements was moving the tractor and trailer on a little so they could throw these branches into the trailer, when Sammie shouted, "Stop," Clements stopped immediately, not knowing what was wrong. Sammie went over and put his back under the side of the trailer, prised it up and pulled out a branch that was under the wheel, threw it up on the load, and said to Clements, "You can go on now." Clements said Sammie would try to lift a piece of timber that would have been too heavy for two men to lift. It all came to a sudden end a couple of days later when they were trying to remove a big ash root. Clements had a good strong steel cable attached from the tractor, around the stump, and back to the tractor again, but the tractor was unable to get sufficient grip, and just sat there with its wheels spinning. "Put the brake on tight," says Sammie. He got a stout crowbar and put it through the centre of the two strands of cable, he then started twisting it round like a tourniquet, and right enough, Clements said he could see the stump starting to come, but after eight or nine turns the pressure was terrific and Sammie's hand slipped during the change over, and the crowbar spun rapidly in the opposite direction, the end of it hitting Sammie's arm and breaking it. Clements took him off to hospital to have it set, and when some of the neighbours went in to the hospital to see how he was. "Well," says Sammie, "Nine revolutions, something had to break."

During the war years, the farmers were obliged to crop their land under the compulsory tillage regulations. Sammie had his few acres ploughed by a local contractor, and after sowing the corn, the whole area had to be harrowed, to cover the seeds, and leave the surface smooth so that it would be easily harvested in the Autumn. Harrowing the ground was a heavy job for which two horses were usually needed, especially on heavy clay soil, but Sammie had just a small pony and very soon the task proved too much for him. He asked a few neighbours if they could lend a horse but all were very busy doing their own work when the weather was dry. So Sammie said to his brother Bob, "Come on here and help Jack out." He harnessed Bob in alongside Jack the pony, and proceeded to harrow the field. At the headland each time, as he reined the team around, he would give the command, "Come round Jack, come round Bob." By evening a very tired team had the job done.

Poor Bob died years before Sammie, maybe the horse work didn't help, he was always chewing tobacco which probably didn't help either. One day Bob and Sammie were going to the bog to cut the annual supply of turf when Bob heard someone squealing. Bob ran in the direction of the squeals to find that a young fellow, locally called 'dummy Drum' had fallen into a bog hole. Bob got a good grip of him, and yanked him up onto the bank, dripping wet. "Have you any baccy," asked Bob. The dummy shook his head. Bob immediately threw him back in again, and walked off in disgust.

At one time the Higgins family had what was commonly known as a 'spade for the bog.' That was a man to cut the peat, one to lift it onto the barrow, and one to wheel it out across the bog and dump it in rows, so it could be spread out later to dry. The third man was their father, but he was now dead, and Bob said, "We miss him terribly, sure he was a great man in the bog." Then when Bob died, Sammie went to the bog alone, and did all three jobs himself. With the removal of each floor of turf from the bog hole the depth went down by about nine inches. After two or three floors of turf were taken out, it was a high step up each time, to empty the barrow. Sammie solved this problem by placing a block of tree trunk about two feet high in the bog hole to step up on so he could climb out. But then he had to continually keep it moved along as he lifted the turf. Sammie thought he was losing a lot of time at this, so he tied the log to his leg with a good strong piece of twine, and had it right there beside him for getting out of the bog-hole each time the barrow was full. But instead of leaving it in the bog-hole, Sammie proceeded to wheel the barrow of turf out over the bog with the log dragging along behind him, all the way out, and back each time.

Sammie was definitely a very strong man. He once told someone that if he had been married, he would have had the country filled with big strong men by now. In conversation he would often comment. "Now that would be a good lift for a man," pointing to some big stone or maybe the front of a tractor. He went to the local cross-roads some times for a chat with some of the local lads, who used to gather there each evening. Tug-of-war was a common pastime for them, and one summer evening the lads were trying their strength at this, when they saw Sammie coming down the road. Alan Wilson decided to have a bit of fun with Sammie, and tied the end of the rope to a small ash tree. Then, standing close to the tree, so Sammie couldn't see what he had done, Alan asked Sammie if he would like to take him on for a pull. Sammie readily agreed, thinking he would have no bother at all pulling him. The rope tightened and Sammie heaved his best, and couldn't understand why he wasn't able to take him, while Alan shouted, "I mightn't take you, but by jove I'll hold you anyhow!" Another night when Sammie arrived at the crossroads, some of the boys told him that Willie Hassard was down at the cross on the previous evening, and had lifted a tree trunk that maybe weighed a tonne. It had been blown down by the wind one night. "Well" says Sammie, "If he can do it, I can do it." Sammie heaved and tugged at it for ages and eventually went off shaking his head and saying. "It can't be done! It can't be done!"

Sammie was cutting some rushes for Alfie Sheridan one

day, and as usual, Alfie brought him some morning tea and bread out to the field, only to find Sammie in an absolute lather of sweat, and him belting away with the scythe as hard as he could. "My goodness," said Alfie, "You seem to have a very bad edge on that scythe. "Ach!" says Sammie, "She's been acting contrariness all morning, and I wouldn't satisfy her to sharpen her." Another time he was helping Alfie to dig the potatoes, and after breaking a spade or two, in the process, to let Alfie see how strong he was. They made their way back to the house at midday for dinner. After finishing the meal they were listening to the one o'clock news, Sammie suddenly jumped up from his chair and went back out to the field without saying a word. Mrs Sheridan turned to Alfie and said, "What's the matter with Sammie?" Alfie followed him back to the field, and asked, "What's the matter Sammie?" "What's the matter, you ask! I'll tell you what's the matter. Did you hear that piece on the news where some fellow was awarded the 'George Cross' for bravery, and not a word about Sammie Higgins who held a madman last night that ten men couldn't hold." Apparently Sammie's neighbour had come home in a drunken rage and was destroying the house when his wife sent for Sammie.

Sammie said that if a man set himself a task, he could see it through no matter how big. He said if necessary he could remove Mullaghy hill with a barrow and spade single-handed. He was coming home one night in his pony and cart, and as he started to descend Mullaghy Hill he noticed that the police were operating a road-block at the bottom of the hill, and he had no lights on his cart. Using his ingenuity he propped the cart against the bank and led the pony round onto the bank and into the cart where he tied his legs with the driving reins, then taking the ponies place between the shafts, he proceeded on down to the police stop. "Why have you no lights on this cart, you know its against the law," said the policeman. "You may ask the driver," said Sammie.

One day he went to William Manley at the nearby sawmill asking for help to build the hay ricks which he had gathered at the farmyard, into a stack or pike for winter use. Unfortunately, William had a lot of timber promised for sawing that day and couldn't help him. "That's all right said Sammie" and went back home. When William had finished the sawing that evening, he went up to see how Sammie had got on. He had a big pike of hay built up, with a big flat stone on the top to hold it down in case it got windy during the night, as he hadn't time to rope and thatch it properly. "How on earth did you get that big stone up there, Sammie," asked William. "I'll show you how," says Sammie, and threw a ladder up against the pike. Up he went and lifted the stone and threw it down. Then he came down and wrestled until he had the stone on his shoulder, and then climbed back up the ladder again with it, and replaced the stone on the top of the pike, saying, "That's how it was done."

The summer of 1950 was one of the wettest in Ireland for a long time, and the farmers just couldn't get their hay dried. When a dry day came everyone was out with pitchforks tedding up the hay in the hope that maybe the next day would be dry also, and the hay could be built up into ricks, or if not dry enough, it was made into laps. These were small bundles, and a really back-breaking job to do. Sammie thought it was better to keep the hay on the move at all times. He went to town and bought himself a complete waterproof suit, saying, "No one could work at hay in this weather without oil-skins." So he dressed up in the oil-skins and tedded his hay, day after day, regardless of the conditions. Needless to say, his hay turned black, and rotted. Some farmers who started very early in June had some good hay, but when the weather broke at the end of June, hay-making became almost impossible. Silage was only made by a small number of farmers at that time, but the Ministry of Agriculture brought in a scheme, subsidising the erection of silage pits and within ten years every body was making silage as the main winter feed for their cattle.

Around about this time, Sammie discovered that motor repair garages were having a lot of used oil to dispose of as the amount of motor vehicles in the county increased. When going into Enniskillen in the car with my father, I recall meeting Sammie with his bicycle heavily loaded with oil drums. There was hardly room for his legs to turn the peddles round. He had a five gallon can tied to each side of the handlebars, and another one tied on the carrier behind him. He was using the old waste oil for a fire, as he had been unable to get the turf dried that year, but dousing them with the oil got them going. The only snag was the used oil was black, and gave off a heavy black smoke when put on the wet turf. Sammie, not that clean at the best of times, got blacker and blacker. One man said, "You would need to spit out, when you looked at him!"

Sammie had a good singing voice, and once appeared on television. It all came about when the BBC decided to do a documentary about the life of Robert Harbinson who was an evacuee in Fermanagh during the war years. He remained on for a few years after the war finished and attended 'Jones Memorial School.' Robert had written a book about the years he spent in Fermanagh, and especially about the Graham family who were his hosts for his latter years there. Sammie was a regular visitor to Graham's also. So he was invited along for the filming, and provided one of his traditional songs.

Desmond Lang told me he had many a great night's crack in Graham's. James Graham was a very quiet wee man, but his sister Lizzie was full of chat and laughs. Hardly a night went by but some of the neighbours went to Graham's for a Ceili. Sometimes, maybe on a special occasion, they would invite a few folks round for a dance. Desmond said he remembered Sammie dancing in the kitchen on the flagged floor, and watched the sparks flying as he did the one step in his hob nailed boots, in time to some music played on a melodeon.

A man over near Bellanaleck went out to the field to fetch his cows in for the evening milking, only to discover that one had slipped into a drain and was badly stuck. This was before there were any tractors to be had, so he went for his neighbour to help pull her out. She was very badly down in a deep drain, and they could make no hand of her at all. The neighbour said," We need to get a lot of help to lift that heavy cow. I'll take my bicycle and round up nine or ten men." When they saw the predicament of the cow, one fellow said. "Send for Sammie Higgins." Sammie arrived while the men were heaving away on some ropes that they had managed to get around the cow. Sammie joined in, and soon the cow was dragged up safely onto the bank. She was little the worse of her ordeal, and the farmer was delighted. "Come on up to the house for a cup of tea," he invited, and before he left, Sammie went over to him and said. "My good man, the next time you have a cow in a drain, just leave your ten men at home, and send for me."

Sammie got a notion into his head one year that there was going to be an Indian summer, and all the water supplies of the entire country would dry up, so he spent weeks digging a huge big pit with his spade. It was about six feet deep by about forty feet long and twenty feet wide. Needless to say the drought didn't come, but Sammie's pit was there to be seen for years, until his nephew filled it in after Sammie's death. Sammie was poor all his life, and not having the money to repair it, his thatched roof eventually fell in. At night Sammie used to crawl in behind a few sheets of corrugated iron, which were leaning against a wall, to shelter from the elements. Then when he was old enough to collect the pension, he used his new found wealth to fix up his house and had a new galvanised corrugated iron roof put on. He was able to save money from his pension, and when he died he left thousands of pounds to the third world.

Robbie

One of the better-known men around Enniskillen was a man called Robbie White. He became something of a legend in his own lifetime. Robbie was a big man, with a large chest and stomach, exactly like the character 'Desperate Dan' from the children's comic, 'The Dandy'. He usually wore leather spats, which made the image complete. He had a large farm about two to three miles from town. He also owned a lorry, which he used for bringing the milk from his farm to the creamery each day. After emptying the fresh milk, he then refilled the cans with buttermilk from the creameries butter making plant, and sold it to the bakeries in the town. Robbie employed three men, to run the farm. Pat Munn, Sam Davis, and John Haire. John was a good worker but saw things in a very simple light. He remarked to someone one day, when they were saying that they had to go into town. "Why don't they build a town out in the country where it would be handy for the people."

As Robbie didn't drive, Pat was appointed to drive the lorry, and he and Robbie could be seen doing their rounds each day. A complaint arose at one of the bakeries, accusing Robbie of diluting the buttermilk with water. The case eventually came to court, and the full story appeared in the local paper, resulting in Robbie being fined. He was at the cattle fair shortly after the court took place, and the local corps of the Salvation Army were holding an open-air service nearby. After delivering his sermon the leader announced the hymn 'Shall we gather at the river,' Robbie who was listening, turned to his neighbour and said, "That's the milkman's national anthem." While Robbie and Pat were driving out home one evening, the lorry ran over something that was lying on the road. The resulting bump caused one of the can lids to jump off onto the road. They stopped the lorry, and Robbie got out to retrieve the lid, but a man had already picked it up. "Did you see a damned lid about?" asked Robbie. "I've got this one," said the Reverend R. J. Good, "But I don't know if it's a damned one or not." Pat and Robbie were trying to park the lorry along the side of the street one day, but didn't have enough space, so Robbie got out and went up to the driver of the car in front of him and said, "Do you play draughts," "Yes I do," the man replied. "Well I moved last. It's your move now." said Robbie.

Before Robbie got the lorry he used to do the rounds with a horse and cart, and when vegetables came ready for harvesting he usually supplied these to some of the townspeople. One day he had John along with him, and a lady asked if he had any rhubarb in the cart. "I'm sorry I haven't Missus," and turning to John he said, "Take this horse and cart, John Haire, return to the farm immediately, and bring this good woman some rhubarb." Meanwhile Robbie went to the nearest pub for a drink and a chat. John arrived back, the horse going at a trot, with a whole rhubarb plant, roots and all, the green leaves of the rhubarb waving in the cart. On seeing it Robbie exploded, "You damned eejit, John Haire, the woman only wanted a few stalks of rhubarb, not the whole bloody plant."

When on his rounds one day a man asked him for the loan of a half crown. Now Robbie had no intention of lending him anything, so he responded, "You have got me on a bad day, I always keep a half crown for that purpose, but the last man who borrowed it, hasn't given it back yet."

One Monday morning he had the workmen lined up, giving them their orders for the day, when a tavelling clothes salesman drove into the farmyard in a small van. Seeing the men in line he got out of his van and stood at the end of the queue. Robbie started with Pat. He said, "Pat Munn, you go and get the lorry loaded, and I shall accompany you to the town later. Sam Davis, you go and get a graip, a barrow, and a hay knife, and proceed to clean out that calf house at the bottom of the yard. John Haire, you go and get the scythe and cut every rush you see in the top field. "Then looking towards the hawker, he said, "And you go to hell." Turning he noticed John was still standing there. "I know what's wrong with you," he said. He went into the house and came back with a plug of tobacco, and gave it to John, who went off with a big smile on his face.

Someone reported Robbie to the labour exchange office, telling them that he wasn't paying one of his men the full agricultural wage, even though he worked hard for him. An official arrived out one day to confront Robbie about this problem. "That is right," said Robbie, "There is one man here that does as much work as the rest of them put together, and gets about half the pay." The official said, "Where is this man? I want to speak to him." "You're speaking to him now," said Robbie. The government appointed advisers who would visit farms and explain the latest ideas, and methods of farming, in the hope of helping the farmers make more profit from their land. One such fellow arrived at Robbie's farm one day, and when he was done explaining, Robbie said to him. "You think you know a thing or two, but I'm telling you I know a thing or three."

Robbie enjoyed a drink at the pub, and one fair day he had a good many drinks with his friends, resulting in him going home in a very intoxicated state. As he made his way home he met his neighbour, Mrs Stinson. "Good evening Mrs Stinson, fresh and well you're looking," he said. "I'm sorry I can't say the same for you Mr White," she countered. "Well, you could if you were as big a liar as I am," he replied. When he was a young man he once took the monthly milk cheque and went to the local pub to drink. Suspecting where he was, his father went to the pub to bring him home. Robbie got him to take a drink before going home, and finished up setting his father drunk. He then took him home and his mother gave the father a good scolding for taking young Robbie to the pub and coming home in such a state.

Robbie always approached a job in a big way and when it was hay-making time he sent Pat into town with the lorry and told him to round up as many men as he could so he could get the hay saved while the weather held. Sometimes he had as many as twenty men in the field putting up about five ricks at a time. He bought a field of potatoes at Kilskeery one time and Robbie who still used horses on his farm, asked my Uncle Ernest, who was his neighbour, if he would bring his tractor and potato digger down and dig them out for him. They left the tractor and digger at the field overnight and came home in Robbie's lorry. Next morning, they were all ready to set off for Kilskeery again to finish the harvesting of the potatoes, but there was no sign of John Haire. "Drive over to his house for him Pat," said Robbie. They were going up the steep hill near John's house when John appeared on his bicycle at the top of the hill. They stopped the lorry to pick him up, but John, having no brakes on his bicycle went whizzing past them down the hill at breakneck speed. He stopped eventually at the bottom and they got him on board. They got the job completed that day without further incident.

Robbie was well on in years when someone made a match with him and a lady from County Kerry. The romance blossomed and soon they got married. Robbie brought her out to Church the next Sunday after they came back from their honeymoon. He introduced her to the Archdeacon, and the neighbours, with the expression. "This is my Kerry-blue." Unfortunately, all romance left the marriage very quickly. After having lived for so long as a bachelor, Robbie found it hard to change his ways, and adjust to married life, and Mrs White returned home to her native Kerry.

Robbie took ill one time and had to go to hospital. Two neighbours were at the cattle mart, and decided to go and visit him. They walked down the ward to where Robbie was lying with his eyes shut. Ernest says to Jack,

"We'll have to come back some other time, he's sleeping." Robbie opened his eyes and said, "I'm not sleeping." "We thought you were, when we saw your eyes closed," said Jack. Robbie replied, "I always keep them closed in here, because every time I open them, I see a corpse." However Robbie pulled through, and started to think about his burial. So he brought the men along to the graveyard, and dug out his grave. He then had it built round with concrete blocks, and filled up with sand so it would be easy to make ready for him when he died.

I'm Telling You Man

About three miles out of Enniskillen there is a high ridge of land over which the road to Swanlinbar passes, known locally as Mullaghy Hill. It was also where the home of William Caldwell was located. I was about ten or eleven years old when I got to know about William. He was probably in his late fifties by then, and to me as a boy, a very old man. He was a well built man who stood about five foot eight inches tall, with a balding head of grey hair, and a handle-bar moustache with the ends twisted and sticking out at each of his cheeks.

My earliest recollection of Willie, as he was known in the local area, was seeing him wheel his bicycle in the lane which led to the Elliott's farm. Most farms had an area of bog allocated to them by the trustees of the ruling landlord of the area, and in Willie's case his plot was just off the side of the Elliott's lane and a short distance from our land boundary. By this time Willie's bog had been all dug over, and the peat extracted for burning on the fire, but the black peaty-soil which remained was ideal for growing potatoes and vegetables. At planting time, Willie could be seen coming in the lane with his spade tied along the crossbar of his bicycle as he made his way to the bog to get his ground prepared and his crop put in.

When we listen to people from the West Indies on T.V. quite a few of them punctuate their sentences with the word 'man.' But Willie was using the expression, 'I'm telling you man' in nearly every sentence years before television was heard of. Often, if he saw my father working in the crop ground which was near to Willie's plot, but on the other side of the Elliott's lane, Willie would come over to have a chat with my father. I would enjoy listening as he emphasised his stories with 'I'm telling you man.'

Willie was very proud of his abilities and often recalled how some big fellow insulted him and they finished up in a fist fight. According to Willie it was a very short combat. Willie said, "I gave him one good skite to the jaw, man, and levelled him out on the road man, six foot two and a quarter man, I'm telling you man."

In his young days, Willie was quite a hit with the ladies and was going out with a girl of ample proportions by the name of Miss Algeo. Some of his contemporaries, not knowing the girl, asked him what she was like. Willie replied, "A big sappy lump, man." That romance fizzled out and he met another girl by the name of Mina Divine who I think came from Tempo and had the qualification of schoolteacher. Willie was reported to have told someone, "My love she is Divine, man." Willie and Mina got married and Mina continued teaching school while Willie continued farming on his smallholding. He told my father one day. "I'm telling you man, I have three good hours hard work done every morning before I get my breakfast, man." My father couldn't figure out what he was doing as he had only four cows altogether.

As well as the four cows, Willie kept a pony to do the carting of farmyard manure, making of the hay in summer, and other light jobs around the farm. In the winter, this pony was grazing in a field near the road, and as grass was not growing at that time of year, the field had become very bare apart from some rushes. George Fawcett, our postman, noticed that the pony had practically nothing to eat, and when he called at the next house he remarked. "I see Caldwell's pony walking around the last rush bush in the field at the cross, I was thinking that he was wondering if he should eat it today, or leave it until tomorrow."

Although Willie and Mina seemed to have had a happy marriage, sadly Mina died quite young, and as they had no children, Willie was left for a long number of years on his own. He had some kind neighbours whom he used to visit most evenings. There he could have a chat and get his evening meal. He missed Mina very much and sometimes in the silence would call out "Mina-man" and occasionally say, "Mina-man, give us a kiss man."

As the years rolled on Willie still put in his vegetable garden in the bog and the talking to himself became more frequent. He was overheard one day having an imaginary conversation with someone about the children, even though he had none, he said, " I'm telling you man, that Willie cub's the divvle man." He had a letter from a nephew in America one day telling him that he may come over to Ireland to visit him. So Willie stuck his spade in the ground and took off his cap and placed it on top of the spade. He then walked back, turned round and stepped over to the spade with his hand out-stretched as in a handshake, saying "Good to see you man." Obviously getting in some practice for the occasion.

Although he was getting frail, he still visited his neighbours most evenings, and in early July he called to visit in a house a bit further away. As he was leaving he noticed some potatoes growing and asked if they were big enough to eat yet. The owner pulled up a stalk, and sure enough there were some small potatoes attached. Willie picked up the four or five of them, saying. "Those will do my dinner tomorrow, man." Next morning there was no sign of Willie and when a neighbour called in to see him, Willie was dead, the potatoes still in his jacket pocket. The farmer later remarked. "I knew by the look of him that he'd never live to eat them."

Hurricane

As one goes through life certain things remain more clearly in the mind than others. People remember something good or bad that made a lasting impression on them. A bad year in Ireland, usually meant a very wet one. 1924, and 1950 were two of these. But 1961 was a year to be remembered because of the hurricane which hit Ireland on the 16th of September. I was at home with my mother when the wind started to increase in strength. Being Saturday morning, my father had gone to town in the car for his weekend papers, as well as getting whatever messages mother wanted for the house, and picking up the meat for Sunday's dinner as he did every Saturday. My eldest sister was married, and my other sister was at work in Enniskillen.

The wind was coming from a southerly direction and as it increased in strength, a gust of increased velocity would bend the trees and move anything that was loose, hurtling leaves, buckets, sheets of corrugated iron, or anything else that was in its path into the walls or hedges around the farmyard. My father arrived home safely about 11am which mother and I were pleased to see. But we had seen nothing yet, as the storm got worse and worse. We had a feeling of helplessness, as we listened to the roar of the wind, and praying that the roof would not be blown off the house. None of us had ever experienced a wind like it. The hurricane continued until about three o'clock in the afternoon, and then it gradually calmed down. We went outside to survey the damage, and although we lived on top of a hill, damage was only slight. We had two or three slates off the roof of the dwelling house, and a sheet of asbestos broken off one of the out houses. The only thing we had to do immediately was to saw up a tree which had been blown down across our lane completely blocking it.

Dad and I got the crosscut saw, and a sharp axe, and proceeded down to where the tree was lying. It was a large sycamore that had been growing on the high bank along the side of the lane. The tree roots had taken the entire bank up on its edge as it fell over. Our terrier dog was intrigued by this new cavern and was soon snuffing around under the tree roots. We pulled the crosscut back and forth, the sharp teeth flicking out the saw dust to each side as we slowly cut our way through the tree trunk, which was about two feet in diameter. Eventually we had it cut through, and whack! The whole bank shot back into its place again. Neither Dad nor I had realised what pressure the tree was counter balancing, and then we thought about the dog. Thankfully he was standing on the lane, ignorant of how in a split second he could have been buried under the tree never to be seen again. As we listened to the news reports on the radio, we realised that we were indeed lucky. Roads were blocked by fallen trees, telephone and electricity lines were down. Buildings had collapsed in different areas and people had been killed. As time went by, stories of narrow escapes, and outright disasters were talked about, and the local newspaper had pictures and stories of the main tragedies. But being Ireland there were also some funny ones. There was a man called John Brodison who lived at Bellanaleck, and was well known for telling tall tales. He said that he looked out of the house, only to see a rick of hay flying by. He said it came all the way from Ballinamore (about 20 miles as the crow flies). When asked how he knew it was from Ballinamore, he replied. "Sure didn't I work there for years, and I know the way they always put the ropes on them."

John worked for William Montgomery on the farm at Clintymullan for a time. William was a man who liked to get on with the job, and John found the work hard going. One Friday evening he asked William if he could have Saturday off as he wanted to go to confession at the 'Graan.' William readily agreed to the request, telling him that he wouldn't keep any man from following his religious belief. Monday morning saw John back to work again, and William greeted him with the remark. "How did you get on at confession, John, did you get any penance to do?" To which John replied, "When I told the Priest that I was working for you, he said that was penance enough." I heard of a man who went to confession one time, and whether his sins were great or not I don't know, but he got a penance to do. The Priest put dried peas into his shoes and told him to walk home on them. He walked about three miles, and his feet got so sore he couldn't go another step, so he called at a cottage of a friend of his by the roadside, and explained the situation. His friend who was Protestant, told him he was a right fool cutting the feet off himself on the hard peas, I would have emptied them out as soon as I was out of his sight. "But," he said, "you don't understand. I must do this if I want my sins forgiven." "Right," says Billy, "Give me those peas." He put them into a saucepan with some water and gave them a quick boil on his open fire. When they had softened a little, he strained them out and put them back into Pat's shoes. "Now," says he, "You can continue in comfort, and no one can say you didn't walk home on the peas."

Billy's home by the roadside, was a place where visitors were always made welcome. Most nights, especially during the long dark winter ones, neighbours would call in for a chat to help pass the time, before going to bed. One night a neighbour came rushing in as white as a sheet, and bust out. "Oh Billy, the devil's after me." He had been walking down the road in the darkness, towards Billy's, when between his own footsteps he started to hear other footsteps following him. He decided to speed up and get away from it, but the faster he went, the faster the footsteps seem to be closing in on him, and now he could hear a chain dragging as well, he broke into a run, and made it to Billy's house, still ahead of the 'devil.' Billy took his lamp and went out of the door, to investigate. Standing there he found a goat with a long chain attached.

It was often debated after the hurricane of 1961, as to whether it was a more powerful wind than the hurricane of the 5th of January 1839. The biggest difference was the 1839 storm came at night, and it was therefore more terrifying. The damage was widespread over the whole country. It became known as "The night of the high wind." A lot of houses in rural areas at that time were little mud-walled cabins with a stone-built chimney. The chimney may as well have been free-standing as the mud walls gave it little support. The strong wind rocked the chimney, and soon it fell over flattening the house as well. My friend Desmond Lang told me he read of a family in County Antrim who were in fear of their lives as the storm raged that night in 1839. Fearing the chimney would fall and kill them, they decided they would have to get out of the house before disaster struck. Taking his wife by the hand they went outside, and then the wife says, "John, what about the gold sovereigns." He says, "I'll go back in and get them." He couldn't let go of his wife as she was small and light, and the wind was taking her off her feet, so he found a piece of rope and tied her to a whin (gorse) bush that was growing nearby. He got safely out of the house with the sovereigns in his pocket, but his wife was nowhere to be found. A mighty gust had uprooted the whin bush, and both it and his wife were blown away, and he never saw her again. Then Desmond said to me. "You know Robert, when I read that I thought it was a pity he didn't tie her to an ash tree, that would have had a good root to it."

The hurricane of 1961 caused a lot of damage, and tradesmen were much in demand for months afterwards. There were still some thatched houses around at that time, and most of them required repairs after the wind had partially stripped them. Once an opening was made, the wind cut deep channels in the thatch as the straws were blown away in a continuous stream. I remember a man, who did thatching, remark that so many people were calling on him to have their thatched roofs repaired, that his house was like a polling booth on election day.

The other noticeable effect on the countryside was the grass on the fields had blackened. Some people thought that there was something unusual borne in the wind that had done it, but I thought it was just the battering that each leaf had to sustain in the strong wind, was the cause. I remembered how George Robinson had blackened the grass as he chatted my father one day for an hour or so, simply by prancing around on it.

The Young Ones

The teenage years are a time for making friends. As we settle into our chosen profession or lifestyle, it is usual to carry on the friendships that were carved out during our school days, and I was no different. Quite a group of us would often get together, and head off to a social, or maybe a local dance. Letterbreen Methodist Hall was always a good place to go for a 'Social.' What we called a 'Social' could possibly be more accurately described as a party. All types of games were played such as, 'The Grand old Duke of York,' 'Last across the mat,' 'The farmer wants a wife,' 'Push the business on,' 'Pass the parcel,' 'Musical chairs,' and 'The waves of Tory.' George Elliott or Robert Wilson usually supplied the music on an Accordion. These were times to meet the local girls, and if a fellow didn't 'click,' then it was usual to hear him remark that the social was no good. The game I enjoyed best was, 'Push the business on.' Each boy took a girl and all formed a circle all holding hands, then with the accordion playing the tune, everybody sang, ["We'll hire a horse and steal a gig, and all the world will do a jig, and we'll do everything we can, to push the business on,"] as we moved into the centre and out again twice. We then clapped hands with the girl on the left, turned and clapped hands with our partner, singing, ["Push the business on, push the business on, and we'll do everything we can to push the business on."] Then holding her in a short hand-grip you swung around with her about seven times, leaving her off on your left. You were then back to the start again but with the next girl in the group. This was continued all round the circle until you were back again to your original partner, and probably feeling a little dizzy from all the swinging.

One night my friend Cecil collected me and a few other close friends in his car and we all went to Letterbreen. But when the social was finished about twelve o'clock, Cecil was nowhere to be seen. We found ourselves completely stranded without any means of transport, and nearly everybody had gone off home by this time. Then Eric came over and told us he had seen Cecil going off in the car, with a girl beside him. "Cecil must be leaving a girl home, come on boys we'll all go over to the dance at Bellanaleck," he said. Off we set on the three mile trek to the village of Bellanaleck, singing, 'Bachelor Boy' and a few other popular songs of that time. After about an hour we had reached Bellanaleck and the dance was going in full swing. One of the big show bands was providing the music, such a contrast to our social at Letterbreen. It had a full drum kit, a trumpet player, a chap on an electronic keyboard, a couple of lads on electric guitars, and a vocalist. They played all the latest popular music of that time, and all the latest dance themes, such as; 'The twist,' 'The hucklebuck,' and of course sang the country favourites. In a break between dances the vocalist did a short funny rhyme, which went like this: "John took Ruth on his motorbike, on the pillion seat sat she, he crossed a bump at eighty-five, and rode on Ruth-less-ly". When it finished a couple of hours later, we still had no way of getting home, except our own two feet. So it was time to retrace our steps over half of our previous journey, as we lived about halfway between Bellanaleck and Letterbreen. We had just turned the corner at Bellanaleck into the road for Arney, when we caught up with Jackie Gault. "No car tonight boys," says he, "Come on we may as well walk on, there's too many of us to get a lift anyway." After chatting for a while Jackie started to sing in his lovely tenor voice, and then to yodel. He did a song called the 'Cattle Call,' Now that was really something! It felt like no time at all, but we had gone a mile up the road. Our musical entertainer was just the job. We reached Arney when the lights of a car appeared. It was Cecil, he had gone home and discovered his brother wasn't home, and surmised that he may be at the Bellanaleck dance. We were delighted to see him because our feet and legs were telling us they had done a lot of walking that night.

In summer time we would take a drive around some of Fermanagh's nice scenic areas, such as the Marlbank Road at Florencecourt, where a beautiful view of Lough Macnean is to be had. We came along the Florencecourt Road one Sunday evening and stopped to chat the four Sheridan girls who were out for a walk. We asked them to come for a drive with us, but they wouldn't come with us unless we took them to town for chips. We readily agreed and later took them back to their house. This was my first introduction to their father, Bertie. The girls all had a ready laugh, but Bertie had the greatest laugh I have ever heard. He would lie back on the settee in the living room, and let big "Yahoo's" out of him that would seem to rock the house. He loved asking us young lads riddles, and roar with laughter at our answers. I remember him asking me, "A man without any eyes went out to view the skies. He saw a tree with apples on it. He took no apples off it, but he left no apples on it. Come on now Robert," he would say to me, a smart lad like you, should know that one. Friendship with the girls continued, we used to bring them with us to socials or dances. We would often be quite late getting back, if we had gone somewhere more distant, but usually went into the house for a discussion on the events of the night regardless of the time. Although Bertie and his wife were sure to be awakened by the noise of our chatting and laughing, he never once complained of being disturbed. On one occasion Angela gave us all cornflakes to eat, probably a gentle hint that it was getting near to breakfast time. It must have been summer time, as I remember driving home without the need for lights. Gradually these days and nights of fun came to an end, as one by one we got married, and settled down.

By this time most farmers in Fermanagh had a silage pit constructed, and the Ministry of Agriculture advisers were urging everyone to cut their grass earlier and get a higher quality feed for their cattle. Instead of cutting the grass in July, or late June, as would have been the case for hay, silage was now cut in early June or even late May. The method had changed also. Instead of mowing down swathes with a mower, for collection by a steel tined buck-rake, the larger farmers had now got a 'Forage harvester.' This machine had a rotor fitted with flails which spun round at high speed, chopping the grass and the wind created was guided up a chute, taking the chopped grass with it into a trailer which was connected on behind the harvester. Today a lot of silage is made by contractors, who come with a team of men, tractors, trailers, and a self- propelled forage harvester, which can clear about one hundred acres or more per day.

A vast contrast from the days of an old fellow nicknamed 'Rattlesnake' who lived in our neighbouring townland of Drumrainey. He was one of the earliest contractors I had heard of. Rattlesnake was a dab hand with the scythe, and could mow two acres per day of good meadow. He was asked to mow a field one time, and the farmer made a bet with him that he couldn't mow it all in the one day. The farmer gave him his breakfast and then Rattlesnake went off to the field, and started to mow. He wasn't mowing very long when he felt the urge to go to the back of the ditch and empty his bowel. In a few minutes he had to go again. The cheating farmer had given him a physic with his breakfast. Rattlesnake soon realised that he would lose his bet with all these stoppages. So he took off his trousers, put a knot in his shirt-tail and mowed away. Not needing to stop now, he won the bet. Rattlesnake lived alone in a mud walled house somewhere in the bog that lies between Derrygiff and Drumrainey. He wasn't quite alone because rats could easily burrow in through the soft peaty ground. Rattlesnake used to make himself a large consignment of porridge for supper, leaving enough over to do his breakfast as well. The rats would come in and eat it while he was sleeping. To keep his porridge safe from the rats, Rattlesnake used to suspend his pot of porridge from a beam with a rope.

One of the most bizarre things to happen at our farm

was a cow calving under very unusual circumstances. It happened after my father had retired. I had to sell off a couple of old cows and the replacement heifers that I was rearing were not yet ready to be taken into the herd, so I purchased a two year old springing heifer from my Uncle. She calved, but was not as good a milker as I thought she would have been. Time went on and I realised she had not been served and therefore not in calf. I kept a close watch on her and one day in July I noticed her standing while another cow mounted her, indicating that she was in heat. I rang for the artificial insemination man to come and she was served with a Hereford bull. This was all normal enough, until she started to show indications that she would soon calve. A week later, in September, she calved, producing a Friesian heifer calf. I immediately checked my records, and had no receipt for her of a December insemination having been done. I then checked with A.I. and they had no record either. My cow had given birth without having been served by a bull. Obviously the insemination done in July with a Hereford bull had no effect as she was already pregnant, and should have been noticed by the insemination man. I told the agricultural adviser who said it was not possible, and suggested that a bull may have got to her without me knowing. This again was impossible because she was tied up in a closed byre from early November, and there wasn't any farmer near us who had a Friesian bull at any rate. Mr How, the vet, was at the farm the following week so I asked his advice on this strange phenomenon. He replied, "If you leave out the sublime, you are left with the ridiculous." I found most people just didn't believe me when I told them, but it was perfectly true. The cow had given birth without having been mated. I have since discovered that only a female calf could be produced, as the bull supplies the male chromosomes, and the further proof was it being a Friesian calf. Someone suggested that two eggs had been fertilised on the previous pregnancy and that instead of producing twins, one had been withheld, but then the first pregnancy was from an Aberdeen Angus bull and not a Friesian.

The Man With Three Thumbs

The part of the townland of Derrygiff presently owned by the Dunn family, and during my young days was the Elliott property, had been previously owned by the Crozier family, who sold it to a newly married man by the name of Frederick Dowler. Fred was a man about fifty two years old when he married his wife Lillian, who was only half his age. After their marriage they came to live on the forty acre farm at Derrygiff. Fred was unique in that he had an extra thumb on his right hand, but his name is still remembered in the area not because he had three thumbs but because of his untimely death. Lillian had emigrated to America as a young girl but had decided to return to Ireland and her native Cavan where she met Fred, who soon became besotted with her attractive looks and outgoing personality.

Fred and Lillian appeared to be very happy at first, and Fred renovated the thatched roofed single storey farm dwelling house at Derrygiff, into a two storey one with a slated roof. Soon Lillian was pregnant, and Fred employed a maid by the name of Jane McPherson, to help Lillian during her confinement. The baby was still born, and over the next six years Lillian produced four more babies, but all were still born. So Fred and Lillian were still alone apart from Jane, and a farm hand called James Willoughby whom Fred employed to assist with the farm chores.

In the small close knit community where everybody knew everybody, gossip soon spread that Lillian and the farm hand, James Willoughby, who was of a similar age, were courting. Jane who was in their company at the house was probably the source of the gossip, as she whispered her suspicions to the women of the area. The alleged affair continued for a considerable time. Lillian and James would go off to Enniskillen, presumably to get groceries and general farm supplies, and were sometimes observed being affectionate, when they thought they were alone. Life for Lillian appeared to be all she could ever have hoped for. Her faithful husband providing her with money to buy clothes, and generally supply all her material needs, while her young lover supplied her physical needs. But suddenly Fred dismissed Willoughby. No one knew why, but maybe he had become aware that something was going on between him and his wife. About six weeks had passed after Willoughby's dismissal, when Lillian Dowler ran to her neighbour's house one February morning in 1939 at about 9.30 am to say that Fred had taken a turn and was unwell. On arriving at the Dowler house, the neighbour and his friend saw Fred writhing in agony on the kitchen couch in a lather of sweat, and said to Lillian, "You may get the doctor at once," to which she replied that she had already sent for him. The two neighbours could hardly keep poor Fred on the couch his convulsions were so great, he had already kicked the end off the couch. Suddenly he reached up and grabbed his wife almost squeezing the life out of her and said,

"Lily don't leave me," She asked one of the men to pull his arms off her, but they didn't have to, these were his last words, he was already dead. Had they been medical men they would have recognised the symptoms as those associated with poisoning. There were no telephones in the area at that time and although a messenger had gone for the doctor about four miles hence in Enniskillen. He didn't get there until after Fred had died. He examined Fred, confirmed he was dead, and strangely diagnosed the cause of death as having been a heart attack. He was duly buried in Cleenish churchyard at Bellanaleck. This was the sudden end of the eventful seven year marriage of Fred and Lillian Dowler.

A couple of days after Fred's burial, Lillian re-employed James Willoughby. The neighbours couldn't help thinking that with Fred now out of the way, they were free to indulge their romance once more. It was just too convenient, and then other incidents began to come to light. Jane McPherson said that after breakfast on the morning of his death, Fred had gone out to attend his cattle, but was very sick and had thrown off his breakfast at the end of the farmhouse. Later on a goose had died after eating some of the vomit, and the neighbours began to think Fred had been poisoned. They had never heard of anyone having severe convulsions for over an hour before dying with a heart attack, but in those days a doctor's word was taken without question. They began to think that Lillian had surely poisoned him, and now that Willoughby was back at the farm, they were even more convinced. Eventually the word reached the ears of the Sergeant of the local constabulary, and he started an investigation. All the neighbours were questioned as to what they knew or heard regarding the affair. A lot of them were strangely quiet about the whole thing, not wanting to get involved in anything concerning their neighbour. Others had no first hand knowledge apart from hearing the local gossip that was rife in the whole locality. My Uncle was cycling down the road on his way from our house to his own home, when he saw them kissing in their lane, as he went quietly past on his bicycle. The sergeant decided that he would apply for a licence to have the body exhumed, and perform an autopsy to see if Fred was, in fact, poisoned.

This was a new phenomenon for the Bellanaleck area that wasn't even a village at that time, just a hamlet, with a church, post office, shop, school, and a couple of houses. The autopsy took place in a farm hay-shed nearby under close police guard. Traces of strychnine were indeed found in several of the body organs and so a full scale murder hunt was launched, with Mrs Dowler and James Willoughby as the prime suspects. The sergeant questioned the suspects, who maintained they were innocent, and couldn't account for how Fred had been poisoned. He then questioned a young man who had been going out with Willoughby's niece. His girlfriend had just recently died of pneumonia but he gave the sergeant some vital information. He said that a couple of months before Fred Dowler had died, James Willoughby had asked him to accompany him to Dowra, some twenty miles away. Willoughby told him that he had gloves to deliver to his girlfriend there, as she had left them behind her when she had last visited with him, and because of the long cycle journey he wanted his company. When they got to Dowra, Willoughby asked him to go along to the chemist and buy some strychnine. He thought it unusual that he should want him to buy the strychnine, and asked him why couldn't he buy it himself. Willoughby said he would be delivering his girlfriend's gloves. On enquiring as to what the strychnine was for, Willoughby told him it was to poison a barking dog that his girlfriend's father kept, so that he and his girlfriend could come in quietly after a late dance without wakening everyone. He went along to the chemist and came back with some rodine which the chemist said would do equally well for that purpose. Willoughby was displeased and said, "Rodine is no good, it must be strychnine." So they returned home without the strychnine, and strangely, without delivering the gloves. The sergeant sent two men to Dowra to check out the story but the chemist there had no knowledge of the incident at all. He went back to his man and asked if he was sure it was Dowra he was in. He said he wasn't sure as road signs had been taken down owing to the second world war plan to confuse any German spies who may be around. The sergeant asked him to retrace the journey with him and discovered that he had a poor knowledge of the country as he had done very little travelling. They set off and he guided the sergeant to Ballyconnell and not Dowra. Sure enough the chemist there recognised the man and collaborated his story. So the sergeant now knew that Willoughby was trying to buy strychnine, but had actually failed to get any. Ironically, his further investigations revealed that Fred Dowler and his wife Lillian had been to a chemist in Enniskillen, to buy strychnine a few weeks before Fred's death. He told the chemist he needed it to kill rats on the farm. The chemist didn't have any in stock, but it was arranged that Lillian would collect it later, which she did. Then on one of his visits to the house the sergeant noticed a newspaper lying on a window sill. On looking at it he saw it was open at an article about poisoning and that cremation of the body destroyed all traces of poison. He also had evidence from the maid, Jane McPherson, who said Lillian and Willoughby were living as man and wife, since the death of Fred, and were openly showing affection for each other. On one occasion they had called her into their room and asked her if she thought they looked well together in bed. The sergeant thought he had enough evidence to bring a case, so he arrested Willoughby and Mrs Dowler on a charge of murder.

The trial took place in December 1939 and lasted for four days at the high court in Belfast, where four hundred people crowded the court room, and hundreds more waited outside to see the accused, and to hear the trial. 'The Derrygiff Murder' was the heading in all the newspapers of the day. On the third day of the trial, the defence established that James Willoughby could not possibly have murdered Fred Dowler, as he was no where near the farm at the time, or indeed for weeks before that. So the case against him was dropped. However the case against Mrs Dowler continued. Several witnesses were called. Some said they had seen Mrs Dowler and James Willoughby cycling to town on numerous occasions. Under cross examination this was un-proven, as the defence pointed out that there was nothing suspicious, or incriminating, about them going to town together. And unless they were actually seen together in town, there was no proof that they went there. Seeing them go in the direction of the town, was not proof that they did, in fact, go to town. Jane McPherson said she had often seen them kissing and had seen them in bed, and that they were living as man and wife. She went on to say that since Fred Dowler's death, she had seen his ghost in the house, and had met him on the stairs, on a couple of occasions. Needless to say the judge hearing the case gave instruction to the jury that Jane's evidence was to be ignored as she was an unreliable witness. My Uncle who testified to seeing them kissing in the lane, had then, the only concrete evidence presented to the court, that there was a romance between Mrs Dowler and James Willoughby. All these things would indicate that they were having an affair but it still wasn't proof that they had, in fact, conspired to murder Fred Dowler. It became known after the trial, that the postman, had also seen them looking out of an upstairs bedroom window on several occasions, when the family dog had alerted them, by his barking due to his arrival with the mail, but he never let the police know about it, so this evidence never came to court.

In his summing up of the case the judge said that the case would never have came to court, only for the gossiping neighbours. Fred Dowler had met his demise by the taking of poison. He may have taken it by accident, or by using a spoon, or cup, which was contaminated with the strychnine, and no evidence was presented before him to prove that Mrs Dowler, had in fact, murdered her husband by poisoning him. So the jury found her not guilty. The case ended with Mrs Dowler being acquitted to rapturous applause from the public gallery. Those who had expected a double hanging were disappointed.

But that was not the end of the controversy, and the murder

charge which had got such publicity. The neighbours who believed she was guilty kept their distance, and soon Mrs Dowler and Willoughby put the farm up for sale. It was purchased by the Neill family and Mrs Dowler and Willoughby went off to a new life in Glasgow. Nothing was heard of them for years until one day the sergeant called into a coffee shop while in Glasgow. The waitress on recognising him asked, "Are you not afraid to eat here, you know I might poison you." She was in fact Mrs Dowler. It was years later while a man was doing some building work for my father on our farm, that we heard something more about Mrs Dowler. He said that, when Willoughby had helped her spend the money they had got from the sale of the farm, that he tired of her, and left her. This was why she was working as a waitress.

I asked my father if he thought Mrs Dowler was guilty and he said, "I believe she was. I don't think Fred Dowler poisoned himself by accident. He had used strychnine for years to poison rats, or sometimes foxes, that would kill poultry on the farm. He knew how dangerous strychnine was, and how little it to took to kill. When he had the strychnine in the house she probably put it into his health salts which he took a couple of mornings a week. Because Fred was violently sick it would indicate that he had taken a large dose and had vomited most of it off, but still enough remained in his body to kill him. Had he got the poison by contamination he may not have been sick." So even though the court had acquitted her, the locals had found her guilty.

Looking back now, I often thought if she had been found guilty at the time, she would have been hanged, and that was the end. But it would appear that escaping the hangman's noose did not bring her happiness, as she lost her friends, and when the money was spent, she lost James Willoughby as well. She probably ended up a very lonely person. How much wiser she would have been to have stayed with her trusting and caring husband. I wonder if her babies were all still born, I think it would warrant investigation by today's standards. Others have said that James Willoughby wasn't her only boyfriend, so the plot thickens. As for the gossiping neighbours mentioned by the presiding judge. Were they not proved right? The murder case also made the previously unheard of townland of Derrygiff, famous.

Australia

Marriage comes for most people at some stage of their lives, and I caught the bug at the age of twenty five. I felt I had had enough of being on my own and it was time to settle down. In the space of five years we had three children, two boys and a girl and life went on much as before on the farm. It was hard work keeping up with the feeding, milking, and looking after the cows, and also attending to about twelve hundred laying hens which was shared by my wife Gretta, but took a lot of time each day. I was always keeping an eye on the profitability of each enterprise, and soon realised the profit margin on the poultry was very bad. So I had a good look at my future prospects in the farming industry in Fermanagh, and came to the conclusion that I needed to buy extra land. This would make my farm viable, and then I realised that I would need to employ help to run it, which in turn would reduce my income. I quickly reached the conclusion that I should change my way of life entirely, and sold my farm and emigrated to Western Australia in August 1974.

From an early age, I had dreamt of going to Australia, it seemed a marvellous place and so large compared to Ireland, it just built up a big adventure in my mind. All that space and sunshine, why wait any longer. I wrote to my brother-in-law, who was a mechanic in a garage in Freemantle, and had a quick reply giving answers to my questions. Being a one man farmer meant that I had to do all sorts of jobs, but I was able to do most things myself. I had often replaced tractor clutch plates, ground engine valves, and repaired hydraulic pumps for neighbours and friends, so I reckoned that I could do mechanic work in Australia. When I got there I found that, without proper qualifications no such jobs were available to me. My brother-in-law had a word with his boss and I got a job in the same garage where he worked, doing the job of pre-delivery mechanic. This involved checking over all the new cars before delivery. It was amazing how many things I found wrong, from the headlights out of line, to rattles, squeaks, broken fan belts, blocked cooling systems, and malfunctioning door locks.

The long journey to Australia was an adventure for us all. We had never flown before, and were especially looking forward to that. The journey started with us all driving to Enniskillen bus station, where I handed over my car to the new owner. We climbed on board the bus that took us to Belfast. On reaching the bus station in Belfast, we transferred to a taxi that took us to the harbour, where we boarded the ferry for the overnight crossing to Liverpool. Our son Ken and I shared a cabin, while Gretta, our son Gordon, and daughter Shirley shared another one nearby. I awoke to find the ferry docking at Liverpool. In a short time we were all up, and ready to leave the ship. We made our way down the gangplank where my brother-in-law Eric was waiting to take us over to his home in St Helens. There we met Gretta's sister Hannah. After a chat and a cup of tea Eric brought us into Liverpool's Lime street station. From there we boarded the train that took us all the way down England to our destination at Euston Station, London. Time for another taxi, this one took us to Heathrow airport, where we got on board the large jumbo jet, that took us to Perth, Western Australia. We stopped at Zurich Switzerland, Bahrain, Singapore, and finally we arrived at Perth after a twenty hour flight. Because of the time difference we were actually into the third day, since leaving Ireland, having used all the modern means of transport, except the bicycle.

So here we were in Australia at two o'clock in the morning, with three young children, and five suitcases that held all our worldly belongings. Some other things that we had packed in wooden cases were coming by sea freight, and were dispatched two months earlier, but as it turned out didn't arrive in Australia until two months after us. Having cleared customs, we made our way to the exit, where Gretta's brother, Tom was waiting for us. He took us over to his sparkling clean Leyland Tasman car. This was the first thing that I noticed on arriving in Australia. Not only was his car sparkling, but all the cars in the car-park were also sparkling. The dry climate meant that roads kept clean and instead of having to wash off road film from the car each week as in Ireland it was only necessary to wash the car about twice a year in Australia. At other times a rub down to remove dust was all that was necessary to keep the car looking great. Tom took us all safely from the airport to his home in Coolbellup, which is a suburb of Freemantle. There we met his wife Rita, and children, Julie, and David. We were all very tired and settled down to sleep in Tom's caravan, that was to be our home until we could rent or buy a house.

My first real look at Australia came next morning, when I awakened and got a surprise to find that the air was rather cool. Being the end of August, and it was also coming to the end of the Australian winter, if you could call it Winter. The temperature rose from about nine degrees centigrade in the morning to about twenty degrees by midday, which I thought was very pleasant indeed. My first impression of the area surrounding Freemantle, was of a barren sandy landscape, overgrown with trees and shrubs. That is, anywhere that hadn't already been covered by house-building. Another thing that got my attention was a continuous clicking sound. On enquiring as to what was causing this sound I was told it was caused by 'Click-Clacks.' This was the name given by the locals to the Australian cricket, which I suppose lived very happily in the rough grass that grew up from the sandy ground. I knew that Irish crickets loved the warm area around the old hearth fires of long ago, and I assumed the Australian cricket was no different, except that everywhere outside was sufficiently warm for them to survive.

On the positive side, the clear blue sky with the sun beaming down, cast shadows of the houses and trees, creating a picturesque series of shapes that moved slowly along as the sun rose in the sky. By mid-morning the little Australian wild flowers had all opened up their petals, giving a most beautiful array of orange, red, yellow, and white to the road verges. Then as the season progressed out came the crimson bloom on the New Zealand Christmas tree, the yellow bloom of the Acacia, and the blue flowers on the Jacaranda. Compared to the deep green of the Irish countryside, Australia's dried out appearance is more than made up for in the marvellous display of colour from its plants and trees.

Arriving in a new country is quite an upheaval for the whole system, getting over jet-lag, new ways of doing things, not knowing where a single road leads to, and when you are in the southern hemisphere one of the most noticeable things is the fact that the sun shines from the north at midday. At least the cars were driving on the same side of the road as they were in Ireland, and although the Holden made by General Motors was probably the most common make, there were plenty of Fords, Toyotas, Hondas, Leylands, and Nissans about, just to mention a few. Most cars were in the larger size with a six cylinder or V-eight engine.

Our main concern was to get a house, and get Gordon back into a school, and Kenneth started in a kindergarten. Shirley was just over two years old then, and still at home with Gretta. We were really glad to have the caravan for sleeping. Tom and Rita gave us the use of their house for eating our meals, and room for the children to play in the garden. But to get settled in properly we needed to get a home of our own. We had been advised to rent a house first, so we could get a feel for the area, before buying a permanent home. In a week or two we found a place and soon settled in. We had a spending spree getting all our furniture, bedding, curtains, and kitchen equipment purchased. It was great to get the clothes which we had brought in our cases unpacked. Other small household things which we had sent on by sea freight still hadn't arrived. While our rented house was very comfortable, and the area a pleasant place to live, I soon realised it wasn't an economical system. We had our money from the farm sale in the bank and we decided it was much wiser to buy a house outright, instead of paying rent. We had another look at what the estate agents had on offer and soon found a suitable house to purchase. It wasn't very far from Tom and Rita, so we still had close contact with them.

At first I felt overdressed with my shirt, jacket, trousers, and leather shoes, when the average Australian was wearing a sleeveless vest, called a tank top, a pair of denim shorts, and open sandals or flip flops on his feet. I actually thought the weather just wasn't hot enough to be stripped down like that, but after a few weeks I got myself a short sleeved shirt and a nice pair of brown shorts, knee length socks, and open sandals. That's how this Irish man looked in Australia.

We hear a lot about the nuisance of flies in Australia, but I was pleasantly surprised by the lack of them in the metropolitan area. There were some, but the most annoying insects were the mosquitoes, which were most active at dusk. Like moths, they are attracted by light, and I had the misfortune to fall victim to a severe biting as I stood in the light of the doorway chatting to the milkman, who delivered the milk in the cool and darkness of the night. I never felt a thing, until I awakened next morning, and discovered my legs and arms were a mass of mosquito bites. I can say with all truth, 'Once bitten, twice shy.'

Generally speaking I found the Australians to be a relaxed, and easy going type of people. I suppose the sunny weather helps to give a holiday atmosphere to the country. Soon I got used to hearing expressions like, 'No worries,' and 'She'll be right mate.' Other expressions were a bit more difficult to get to grips with. I had to have the term, 'Bludger' explained. This is Australian for a lazy person. I was fascinated by the name 'Bluey' given to red-haired people. The explanation here is that they have blue eyes. English immigrants were given the tag, 'Pome.' pronounced, 'pommy' The explanation being that early immigrants were 'Prisoners of Mother England,' and had the letters P-O-M-E printed across their shirts. Italian's were nicknamed, 'Dings,' This is derived from the old Italian legend of Romulus and Remus being abandoned, and being reared by a she wolf. The nearest thing in Australia to a wolf is the wild dog or Dingo, and the Australians shortened everything that could be shortened, hence 'Ding.'

Compared to the Ireland that I had left, Australia was a very cosmopolitan society. The majority of people were of British descent, but there were a lot of Italians, other Europeans, Asians, and native Aborigines. I found them to be generally helpful and friendly, but their lifestyle was so different to what I was accustomed to in Ireland. Come Saturday, Gretta and I would take the children with us to the shops to buy the weekly groceries, and whatever else was needed, in the house. Then spend the afternoon at the beach or tidying the garden, or mowing the lawn, which was usually a monthly event. Most lawns were planted with buffalo grass which was strong and tough, and could withstand the hot dry Australian climate very well, but it still required watering at least twice per week to keep it looking good. An Australian colleague told me I was mad. He said, "What you need to do, Bob, is throw her a few dollars, and you go along to the pub for a few beers while she gets your eats, and let her call for you there when she is finished." I thought this was a terrible way to treat one's wife and not being a beer drinker I continued with my Irish style. My Australian friend would have done as he advised me and then spent the afternoon either watching horse racing on the television or back at the pub and maybe putting a few bob on a horse. Sunday was his day for cutting the lawn, whereas we would have been off to church. Of course, some Australians would have done similar to us and have gone to their place of worship on Sunday also.

My first job as pre-delivery mechanic came to an end quite suddenly. The garage where I worked had the agency for Leyland cars and the company in Australia had made a new model called the 'P76.' It was not selling well, and I could see why. It was a large ugly car with a boot that could be closed with a forty gallon barrel inside, but because of lack of appeal, and therefore poor sales, the cost of production could not be met and so the company went bankrupt. This came back to me in the form of, no sales, no need for a pre-delivery mechanic, last in, first out, so out you go Bob. (As I said the Aussie's shorten everything, including my employment.) Even though I was only about three months working as pre-delivery mechanic, I can now look back on it as a time of great learning about Australia and Australians generally. Also the different attitudes of each nationality, as I had daily contact with them. I could see the confusion of the foreman by my honesty. I quickly realised he was used to employees trying to lie their way out of a difficult situation first, before finally having to admit it was their fault. To give an example of this, I had a radio to fit in a new car one day, and while using the hole-saw to cut a hole in the wing for the antenna, I had the mishap of it going through the thin steel of the car much quicker than I had expected, with the body of the drill striking the paint work of the front wing resulting in a score in the paint around where the radio antenna was to be secured. When Bob the foreman saw the damage he asked me if I had caused it. I readily admitted that I had. He was speechless by my honesty. Eventually he said, "this will have to go to the paint shop for repair." I was eager to see how the job would turn out, and when the car came back I quietly made an inspection and was greatly relieved, it was excellent, not a sign of the scratch was visible.

I remember Bob telling us one day, that he had a small workshop and petrol station of his own at one stage of his life. It was the custom in Australia to close for the weekend, while a roster system kept fuel supplied to the public. Bob said, "I wound on the pumps about ten cents a litre," being on roster, and therefore the only fuel outlet for miles around, business was brisk, and the money rolling in. He said it wasn't until next evening that someone spotted his high price. "How on earth did that happen," said Bob, "I'll have to get these pumps seen to first thing in the morning." The garage had a main workshop, and then a lean-to with open frontage. I worked in the first bay of the lean-to doing the checks on the new cars. Next to me was an English chap, originally from Liverpool, doing car servicing, and at the other end was a Polish chap who did lubrication and greasing.

One day, the Lucas salesman called, but his contact in the office was out, so he came out of the office to wait for him. When I heard him speak I immediately recognised his Northern Irish accent, and went over to say "hello" to him. "You sound like a man from Ireland," I said. "I am indeed, from Ballymena in fact, where are you from?" I replied, "From Enniskillen." He said, "Sure my wife's from there, she used to work for the 'Impartial Reporter' newspaper." "Is your name McClure?" I asked. "It is, how did you know that?" "Well," I said, "My cousin John has a girlfriend who works for the 'Impartial Reporter,' and before I left Ireland he gave me your address thinking that maybe someday I could look you up." We could hardly believe it. In the midst of hundreds of thousands of people that we should meet like this. I told him that another Fermanagh couple lived near him and later on, I learned that they had made contact, and that their wives had become firm friends.

Within a week of leaving the garage I had a new job, this time I was working in a factory producing all sorts of cans, from the smallest coke can right up to the large gallon sized oil cans. I was at the start of the production line where the tin sheets freshly painted with the details of the ultimate contents, were cut into the sizes required. It was a very monotonous job pushing those thin razor sharp sheets, into pre-set cutting wheels to be sliced to size and then placed on a pallet for collection by forklift truck and taken to the next stage in the manufacturing process. By this time, the Australian summer was with us and soaring temperatures came with it. The heat of the sun on the corrugated galvanised iron of the factory's walls and roof, some days reaching 106 degrees Fahrenheit, and the noise of the machinery as it clanked out the bases and lids for the cans made it a rather unpleasant place to work.

After about three months I changed to a new job. It came

about in an unusual way. I was mowing the lawn one Saturday when a voice from over the fence called out, "Hey mate, did I see you at Church last Sunday." I said, "Yes, you probably did," and we chatted for a while as he explained that my neighbour, was his sister, and that he came from Scotland originally. Eventually he asked me what sort of work I did. He had been thinking of changing his job, but when I told him of the conditions in my work place, noise, heat, and clock-in, wages etc, he told me I should try for a job in Coles warehouse. You have no clock-in, more relaxed conditions and better pay.

I made my way to Coles for an interview on the next Tuesday, armed with a couple of references I had got before leaving Ireland. One of the company directors was on hand to interview the twenty or so men that were queued up when I got there. Eventually my turn came. On reading the reference given to me by the Reverend Alan Hanna. The interviewer asked me if I got the job would I intend staying at it, as he was fed up taking interviews. I said yes I would. He then said, "Okay give me your phone number and I will let you know if you have been successful." I was quite surprised when he rang to tell me I had the job, as I later learned that one of the other applicants was a cousin of the foreman.

My new job with Coles / K-Mart was in a former wool shed. These sheds were originally built to store wool for export from the docks at Freemantle. There were in two rows of ten individial buildings, of uniform size, with walls of concrete up to eight feet and topped by corrugated iron up to the top reaching about twenty feet high in total with a corrugated iron roof. The floor area was three hundred feet long by about one hundred feet wide. The wool trade must have been in decline as most of these sheds were now being used for other purposes. The shed had a large door at each end, and we had a continuous flow of lorries, or trucks, as the Australians called them, coming in at one end, down the centre isle and out at the other end. About four fork lifts were in use all the time unloading the incoming ones, and loading empty ones to take the full pallets of supplies to the twenty five or so stores the company had in Western Australia. Some had to be sent by train to outlying places such as Kalgoorlie, Albany, and Geraldton.

The office staff consisted of two women, and Stan the foreman. Twenty men were employed packing the pallets with cartons from the rows of racks which were laid out along each side of the shed. I started off doing this work. Armed with a list of requirements and a little hand drawn trolley, with a wooden pallet on it. I went around picking up the cartons, ticking off my list and building them on the pallet for collection by the forklift. It was a bit soul destroying and monotonous, but steady work and after a month or so I got a promotion to what was referred to as the 'paper and string' department. I was then working alone in a section that supplied labels, wrappings, bags, in fact all the day to day requirements for the stores that were not for sale, but used in the running of the store.

Tea breaks of about fifteen minutes were at 10am, and 3pm, with a forty five minute lunch break at 12.30pm. These times were an education in themselves. Of the twenty employees, we had a Sicilian, an Italian, a

Canadian, a Dutchman. Another chap and myself from Ireland, four from England. The rest were probably second or third generation Australians, and one fellow who was part Aborigine. No matter what topic came up, someone had a first hand knowledge of it. Soon after I started work there another chap called White came on the staff. He had served with the Australian army in Vietnam and supplied vivid accounts of the action, on and off duty during his time there. He was an avid player of the board game 'Draughts' and was keen to get us involved in a game during our lunch breaks. No one was volunteering, so I said, "I'll play a game with you." So next day he arrived with his draughts board and he and I settled into a game when we had our lunch taken. Most of the other men sat around the table watching as the game progressed. I tried all my skills to manoeuvre him into a position so I could take his men and could hardly believe it when I eventually won the game. Some of the onlookers applauded me with words like, "Well done Bob," and to my opponent, "I thought you were an expert player." Poor White was downcast at the result, and said, "I've got the measure of you now Bob, and you will never beat me again." We played every day for the next week and sure enough I never won another game, and none of the other lads would offer to take him on, so that ended the draughts playing.

It is great to experience all the attitudes of the different nationalities and their individual thinking and styles. We had a fellow who was living in Australia for a couple of years and thought he knew more than anybody else. No matter what subject came up he had the answer. He was soon nicknamed 'The Professor.' Strange to say most of us didn't believe the half of what he said anyway, so his unsolicited ranting mostly fell on deaf ears.

Then there was Joe. He had a pale wrinkled face, probably from the sunny weather and maybe dehydration, accelerated by his heavy drinking of alcohol. He proudly recalled that he lived for a while in Brazil and had drunk a bottle of whiskey each day. I said to him, "You must be an alcoholic," to which he replied, "Not a bit harm it did me." Needless to say he spent every evening drinking in the pub which made me think he was probably unaware of his addiction. I got along well with the staff at Coles, and felt a little lonely when I handed in my resignation one day. Gretta and I had had enough of the blazing sun, and were missing our Irish friends and relations. We decided that after two and a half years, we would return to Ireland. For fun I gave my resignation in rhyme to the office girl, who in turn past it on to head office.

It went something like this:-

My time has come, to resign,

I leave for Ireland in two weeks time.

Australia has been good to me,

I've enjoyed the chat, the fun, the sun,

but now my working here is done.

I may return, one never can tell.

To all at Coles I bid farewell.

Apart from the daily work in Australia we had lots of free

time to enjoy the nice weather and visit places of interest. King's Park is a fabulous place to spend a day. It has an area of about a thousand acres of high ground on the edge of Perth city. From the park a most marvellous view is to be had. You can see the tall skyscraper buildings of Perth. Look down on the sweeping highways that run along the banks of the Swan River. The river here is about half a mile wide, and makes a marvellous spectacle as it makes its way to the Indian Ocean. Most of the park is natural gum forest, palm trees, and grass, but a considerable area is laid out in beautiful flower beds, ornamental landscaping, water features, and a restaurant. Our friends Jim and Louie Martin first took us to see the park a few weeks after we arrived in Australia. Jim and Louie had emigrated from Fermanagh a few years earlier and were settled into the Australian way of life.

Another large part of our life was taken up with the church. Although most Australians didn't seem to worry to much about spiritual things, some did attend church. Those who did attend were mostly very enthusiastic, and joined in all the activities afforded. We had great times with a group called Y.A.M.S. The initials stood for 'Young adults married and single.' We had a really marvellous evening at Coogee park on our first Christmas Eve in Australia. With a temperature of around ninety degrees Fahrenheit we sat around in a circle singing Christmas Carols. Then as dusk came and daylight faded, we lit up candles and continued our singing. It created a lovely atmosphere. It was such a contrast to Christmas in Ireland, and gave us a strange feeling as we did our celebrating in the Australian Summer.

We made many friends through church but our special friends were Jim and Hazel Creagh. Hazel was church secretary and Gretta found a lot to talk to her about including child rearing, their children being just a couple of years older than our three. Jim on the other hand talked very little but I found that we had something in common in our love for machines, especially old tractors. Jim had also been reared on a farm. A completely different type of farm to the one on which I had been reared. His farm was a large wheat and sheep station about two hundred miles east of Perth. Jim said life on his farm was easy for most of the year except for the seed sowing period. They had to wait for rain to come and then the ploughing had to be kept going right round the clock. This was to get the seeds in while there was still sufficient moisture in the soil to ensure germination. Western Australia's farmers led a precarious existence depending completely on rainfall. Jim said if you could get eight inches of rainfall in the season you could grow wheat. Trouble was that some years they didn't get it and had a crop failure. Then on a high rainfall year they would have such a good crop that they were financially secure for the next three years. Jim told me he was heartbroken at having to leave the farm. He had got married, borrowed money to build a house, and then unfortunately got three bad seasons in a row and the bank refused to loan him any more money, so he had to sell up and move into the metropolitan area where he got a job delivering oil with a tanker. On the brighter side he had savings from the farm sale that meant the family was now financially secure.

One of the highlights of my friendship with Jim was a visit to the neighbouring little town of Northam to see a rodeo. I had never seen a live rodeo and we set off one morning to drive the eighty miles or so to see the spectacle. As we travelled along, I observed a large steel pipe of about twelve inches in diameter that was laid a few metres back from the roadside. Jim explained that it was the water main which supplied Kalgoorlie with drinking water from a reservoir in the hills near Perth. I knew that Kalgoorlie was several hundred miles away, and commented that it must have been quite a engineering achievement back in the eighteen hundreds when modern tools would not have been available. Jim said that an Irishman by the name of C. J. O'Connor who was an engineer had the idea to supply water to the gold mines of Kalgoorlie. The area around Kalgoorlie had very little water apart from some underground wells. He estimated that the supply reservoir near Perth was sufficiently higher than Kalgoorlie and that water could be supplied by gravity. A strong opposition to his opinion arose. They said that water would not travel the undulating ground as air locks would stop the flow. C. J. managed to get his idea approved by the government, and a pipeline made from wooden boards held together with steel hoops and water proofed with pitch was laid. (This has since been replaced by the present steel one) Eventually the pipeline was finished and C. J. had estimated it would take two weeks for the water to reach Kalgoorlie. The two weeks came and went, still no water. Three weeks passed, and C. J. O'Connor decided that indeed the water wasn't going to arrive. In despair he went down to the beach at Freemantle and took his own life. Ironically the water did arrive in Kalgoorlie three days later. The people of Western Australia erected a monument to his memory, and as a tribute to his work. His statue stands on the harbour at Freemantle.

We arrived in the small market town of Northam to find a large gathering of people standing around a circular arena where the action had already started. At one end some holding pens held wild ponies, bulls, and calves. Jim and I took up our positions at the rail, and I proceeded to capture the scene with my cine camera. It was just like a scene straight out of a western film. Guys with large cowboy hats mounted on wild horses would come bucking out of an enclosure near the holding pens, and gallop madly round the ring, while taking huge jumps into the air, all four legs leaving the ground. The rider doing his best to stay in the saddle, while being cheered on by the crowd. He lost points if his hat came off, and he had to stay in the saddle for a minimum of ten seconds to claim a valid ride. If successful, a big cheer went up, but most of the riders were thrown to the ground before they were half way round the ring. How they got up and walked off amazed me. Maybe these people were made of rubber. Next came the bull riding. These mad creatures had a rope secured around the rib area, just behind the front legs. This was all the rider had to hold on to as he rode bare-back. The animal bucked wildly. First front end and then the rear end would go up as the gallant rider held on with one hand. Then the scene changed slightly as the commentator announced it was time for the bull-dogging. This procedure started off with a calf about one and a half years old being released into the arena while a cowboy came galloping alongside, on a trained horse this time. His aim was to jump off the horse close to the calf and with his arm around the calf's neck he had to bring the animal down and bind it's four feet with a rope, as the cowboys do for branding. Needless to say only two out of about ten who tried, were successful in completing this manoeuvre. At short intervals in the programme we were entertained by a couple of guys dressed up in circus outfits and carrying colourful umbrellas. They would move up to a bull and poke the umbrella at the bull as they got closer. The bull would give a snort and charge at them. Luckily they always seemed to have the agility to side step each charge, to the delight of the crowd. I reckoned they were getting that matador feeling. I would have certainly not wanted to swap places with them. The Northam Rodeo finally came to an end and I think it was the one event I would have hated to have missed even though the folks taking part must have been a bit soft in the head to put themselves in such danger.

We were over two years in Australia when we decided to return to Ireland. Strange to say it was the sunny weather that had attracted me to go there, and also the sunny weather that made us decide to leave. We had had enough of the strong burning sun, day after day. We also felt that the children were being deprived of knowing their grandparents. So back we came to Enniskillen.

Retail Trade

Returning to Ireland was also a big move. We had to sell off all our household equipment and furniture, only bringing home what was of personal value and essential use. I recall going to the shipping agent in Freemantle for advice on packing and shipping. As the only breakages we had on the outward journey were the items that were repacked by the shipping line in Belfast, we saw no difficulty in doing the packing this time ourselves. The very efficient dispatch clerk gave me the necessary details, and what size to make my packing box. I got the wood and made a box about two metres long by one metre high and one metre wide, with two pieces of evenly spaced wood around the outside making a clearance of three inches so that a fork lift could get under it no matter which side was up. Gretta and I packed all our valuables carefully inside, putting our most delicate china in the centre, so that it was under equal pressure no matter which side of the box was up during transport. When we had our house sold and the date set for leaving we put an advertisement in the local newspaper advertising all our furniture and household effects which were too big and expensive to ship home. When the paper came out and people read of our sale they came round to the house in a steady stream all day, and by the time I got home from work, Gretta had all sold except for a small oil heater. But before bedtime a woman came and bought it too. We had to make arrangements to keep our beds and kitchen table until the day before we left. I remember I made a present of a large screwdriver and my hammer to our friend Jim Creagh. You see I couldn't put them into the box because I needed them to fix down the lid. All safely arrived at my sister's house in Ireland about four weeks later.

We had purchased a house on the Sligo Road at Enniskillen before we left Australia, so it was waiting for us to occupy, and after some painting and wallpapering we moved in. We had left Australia when the temperature was around ninety degrees Fahrenheit and here we were in Enniskillen shivering at the end of October in a temperature of around forty. We had a big spending spree, fitting out our new home with carpets, curtains, and furniture. Then I had to find work. Strangely two jobs came my way, and both were offering me the same wage. The first one was the position of fitter for a company selling milking machines and milking parlours. The other one was fitting curtains and blinds for a local shop in Enniskillen. I was undecided as to which one to go for, until I met with a neighbour, who strongly advised me to do the curtains and blinds.

So began my time in the retail trade. Mr Wilson quickly told me the work was variable, measuring and fitting curtains and blinds, some jobs would take all day and others would maybe involve putting in three screws in three minutes...I never did manage the three screws in the three minutes. There was always something unexpected to deal with. Maybe the spot where I had to drill over a window had a metal reinforced lintel, and had to be done with a separate drill, or there was no firm place to secure the curtain track to. However I soon settled into the job, and enjoyed travelling to the different houses erecting curtain tracks, hanging curtains, or fitting blinds. I was once called back to a house where I had hung curtains the previous day. When I arrived the lady went through to her kitchen after telling me to go into the living room and look at the curtains and see if I could find anything wrong with them. I did as she asked and gave them a thorough examination. Finding nothing wrong I went to her in the kitchen. "I can't find anything wrong with the curtains," I said. "Did you not see one side longer than the other one." In despair I said, "I'm sorry I can't." "Well get down on your knees and look at them and you will see it." Sure enough when I went down to floor level I noticed that one side was about a quarter of an inch longer than the other side. The repair was very simple, just stretch the short one with a good pull, but I couldn't do that with her watching, so I had to take them down and bring them back to the shop where we give them the necessary stretch and refitted them the next day to her complete satisfaction.

Mr Wilson had a good reputation for supplying curtains and got some large contracts for the making, supply, and fitting of curtains in various schools throughout Fermanagh. This kept me well employed making the heavy duty pelmets from four inch by two inch timber, painting them, and taking them to the schools where I had a heavy job fitting them above my head in the large windows. While working at a secondary school one day a class of boys were playing cards when the teacher was called away from the classroom. One of the boys in that class appeared to be beyond discipline. While the teacher had some of the other children reading aloud from their text book about a dog, he would interrupt with comments, such as. "God, he must be a powerful smart dog, I wonder where I could get one of them, I could make a few pound with him." The teacher told me afterwards that they could make no hand of him at all and just ignored his remarks.

When the shop wasn't busy I sometimes took the sales van up to the family house and gave it a wash. Mrs Wilson usually invited me in for a cup of tea on these occasions. It was also a change from the curtain hanging. But not all jobs were pleasant. The worst case I encountered was a lady....or should I say tyrant who lived at Derrylin. She had ordered some curtains for two windows in her drawing room, and when the dressmaker had them made I took them out to fit them. She had chosen a thick tweed cloth and when I got one window fitted she arrived into the room to look at them. She picked up a curtain and said, "What kind of a mess is that, who ever saw a big thick wad of cloth doubled up like that, sure that's no way to hem curtains, you can take them back to the shop and make that a single hem." I had been standing quietly listening to her tirade, and now said, "That's all right, I'll tell the dressmaker to alter them for you," took down the curtains and brought them back to the shop. A few days later I arrived back with the curtains and hung them up again. She went over to them and said, "Those are still not right, look at the way they are hanging." I said, "That is because they are heavy tweed and they always curl out at the bottom when newly hung, but that will straighten out after a while." "I tell you, I'll straighten you out, and take your blooming curtains out of my sight before I break a chair over your back, and don't come back here until they are perfect, DO YOU HEAR ME." Well I said no more, just packed up the curtains and headed back to the shop, but my troubles were not over, before I reached Enniskillen I met a car, which flicked a small stone which happened to be lying on the road, right across my windscreen, shattering it into a million bits. What a day! I slammed on the brakes and slowed down but couldn't see out until I poked a hole in the shattered glass. I slowly made my way to the shop and told Mr Wilson what had happened. "Don't worry Robert, I'll take care of this now, you shouldn't have to take that kind of abuse from anyone."

Other times in the shop we had the best of fun with the odd joke being told and everyone getting on with their individual task. It was my job to open up the shop at nine o'clock each morning, and to lock up again at six in the evening. Customers didn't usually start arriving until nine thirty or ten a.m, so that spare time was usually spent tidying up the department and sorting out the jobs for the day. I remember Gladys, the lady in charge of the department, looking at a pair of curtains that had just been made by the dressmaker, and wondering how they would look when they were hung up. I said, "That's no problem at all," and jumped up onto the counter, picked up the curtains and suspended them at arms length for her to see them properly. The effect was unimaginable on her, she flew into an absolute panic in case someone came into the shop. "Get down off that counter, Robert, you should never do the like of that," she exclaimed. Two of my longest trips were to Belfast and Dungannon, these occurred during the annual sale when supplies had to be replenished owing to the huge demand for the cheaper stock. The sale was a big event in the life of the shop. It took place about the end of January each year when most other shops were finished with their new year sales. The shop was filled to capacity with all sorts of drapery items at half price or less. The curtain department also carried bed-linen and other household items so the whole area was stacked with sheets, pillowcases, bedcovers, duvet's etc.

One evening, a neighbour of mine arrived into the shop just before closing time. I had been out fitting some curtains and found her waiting to see me. "Can you give me a lift out home Robert," she asked. We made our way out and as I was going to the car she said, "I have some stuff that I bought at the mart being kept for me at the bus station. Over we went to the bus station and I could hardly believe what I saw. She had a young tree about six feet tall to bring home. I picked it up and as I walked along the top of the tree rippled along the corrugated roof of the bus station veranda. I laid down the back of the passenger seat and put the tree into the car, with the potted roots in at the passengers feet, while the rest of the tree stretched all the way back to the rear window. I got my neighbour in behind me and off we set. Arriving home we got all safely unpacked and I got a laugh when she broke wind with a loud crack. "Excuse me Robert," said she, but you can't stop wind.

Before the shop opened on the starting morning of the

sale, people were queuing up outside. Then when it commenced, all the staff were going at full speed until closing time. This was a time when I joined in with the selling, as another pair of hands were welcome. The sale was usually for a period of ten days, and probably brought in a good income for the shop. I was just about a year in the shop and realised that my wage packet was not enough to sustain my wife and growing family. I asked for a raise but was told there was no way it could happen, so I resigned and got a new job after a few weeks selling animal feed to the farmers.

The Nut Traveller

I was feeling slightly apprehensive, as I drove in my Ford Escort towards Strabane, to start my new job as a salesman for Smyths animal feeds. I was the new representative for the company, and my area was all of County Fermanagh. Because of my farming background, I knew about farming and feeding animals, but was unsure if I could persuade farmers to buy the product. This requires a particular personality, and explanatory skill, but anyway I was willing to give it a try. My other problem was my back. I was just getting over a bad bout of sciatica and I was still very sore when I moved. Getting in and out of the car was difficult but once I had gone a few miles, the ache eased off, and I was okay. In about an hour I arrived at the office in Strabane, and was introduced to the other members of staff, as they came along. During my initial interview for the job, I had found Mr Smyth to be a pleasant man with an English accent, which took me by surprise. I later learned that he was educated in England and had picked up the accent then.

After my initial introduction to the office staff, Mr Smyth told me that Sam would take me round the existing customers where he would introduce me to the farmers, and show me what the job entailed. Sam who had got a promotion, and was the previous traveller for Fermanagh showed me around the mill, and explained each part of production to me as we went along. It was time to get on the road. Sam took me off with him around the Castlederg and Sion Mills area that day, giving me a first hand experience of how the job was done on the ground. We visited numerous farms where we were made very welcome, and Sam did out the receipt, and accepted payment for the previous months deliveries. That was my first day over and it went very well, but the next day was going to be different. Sam arranged to meet me at Lisnaskea cattle mart. He had a little wooden office there, where he met the farmers, and transacted business as they visited the mart. I arrived in good time and was waiting for Sam when a well dressed man carrying a plastic bag came along. He didn't appear to be all that happy to see me, but he did manage to say, "You must be the new man." I said, "Yes I am," and we said very little more until Sam arrived. Sam said to me with a smile, "I see you have met Stewartie." Stewartie was a little apprehensive about meeting me, the new guy, as he worked for the company in Tyrone, and only came to Fermanagh on Tuesdays and Thursdays to assist Sam. I suppose he felt very unsure about how he and I would get along. After a while, the ice started to melt and I felt a little more comfortable. I later learned that Stewart had a suspicion, that I was going to steal over some of his customers. Of course I had no intention of doing anything of the like, but he had that problem with another one of the travellers, who was no good at his job, and tried to switch over some of Stewart's customers to his account. This meant that he would get the monthly commission from the farmer's purchases while Stewart did the work.

Most of these were small farmers, and the average order was about half a tonne of feed, made up of different types, which was delivered next day by the company lorry direct from the mill in hundred weight hessian bags. A steady stream of customers came into the little office, paid their last account and placed an order for their new delivery. Some men liked to chat for a while or talk about the latest football match. One man always had a joke or yarn to tell us. I found them to be quite a friendly group generally, even though some of them could strike a hard bargain, saying the meal was too expensive, and another company was offering the same feed for pounds less. This infuriated Stewart, his face would flare up red, and with his eyes popping, he would thump his fist down on the counter, saying, "But it's not the same feed at all, I tell you, they are putting cheap by-products into their feed, and you won't get the same results at all. What's the use of selling at a lower price if the quality is not in it, it will cost you more at the end of the day." Months later when I was getting to know the customers on a more personal level, a man said to me, "You know Robert, I tell Stewartie I can buy cheaper just to hear him ranting on about the high quality feed he's selling."

After the cattle sales finished in the mart around two or three o'clock in the afternoon, and the farmers started dispersing Sam and I set off in his car visiting the larger farms where the meal was bought in bulk. That meant deliveries of four tonnes or more, which was delivered loose in a special lorry that had a blower for putting the feed into a bulk bin on the farm. It became the normal practice to call with these farmers after the twentieth of the month when the monthly milk cheques had been received, and there was cash in the kitty. We did the Newtownbutler area on the Tuesdays and around Rosslea area on the Wednesdays. Thursday was the market day for Enniskillen and Sam had a little office there too, just inside the entrance gate. The Enniskillen Cattle Mart was the largest in County Fermanagh and sales went on all day until about four in the afternoon. We took turns in going across the street to the Railway Hotel for our midday meal and usually finished work when the mart closed, unless there was something urgent to attend to.

When I had met most of the existing customers, and was feeling much more confident about what I was expected to do, Sam left me to my own devices. I was the new traveller, and as well as me getting to know my customers, they had to get to know me. Selling the feed was no problem at all that first winter. People phoned me up at night to place bulk orders and new customers called into the mart office. Everything was going great, well would have gone great if the mill had been able to deal with all the new business. It wasn't because I was a great salesman but because it hadn't been a good summer. Hay and silage were both scarce and not of good quality. Farmers found that buying the manufactured concentrates was cheaper in the long run because they got good results. However it didn't last for long, as the mill became overloaded with orders, delivery became slower and one morning a distraught farmer rang me up on the phone to complain that his order had not been delivered, and he was almost out of feed for his cows. I phoned the mill immediately and asked to speak to the sales manager. He was a man nearing retirement, but had instant recall of all the orders that were currently in the process of being delivered. When I said the farmers name and that his meal wasn't delivered, he promptly replied. "He has no meal on order, it's dairy nuts he gets." I said. "Sorry, I know it's nuts he gets, it was just a figure of speech." "Well you better have it right, you know there is a big difference between meal and nuts. Yes, that order is going out tomorrow morning." Later, when I met up with Sam again, he had a good laugh after I told him of my rebuke from the sales manager. "He's on the ball right enough, and can be a bit gruff at times, but keep on the right side of him and you'll be all right," he said. "But you see Sam," I explained, "I was only using a figure of speech, when I said his meal wasn't delivered. I would refer to myself as a meal traveller, but I'd never refer to myself as a 'NUT TRAVELLER'.

During the school summer holidays my children used to come with me occasionally on my rounds of the farms. Only one was allowed to come at a time. Gordon, who was always very active, didn't come with me very often, as he got bored waiting in the car while I chatted with the farmers. Instead he got himself a summer job, cleaning boats at a marina near home. Ken, who liked to pull an occasional prank on me, looked forward to a day out around the farms. I pulled into a farmyard one day, stopped the car, and as I got out, I was suddenly jerked back onto the seat. Ken had tied my anorak strings to the car seat-belt. He had done it so delicately as we drove along, that I never felt or knew a thing, until I tried to get out. He had a good laugh at me. Another time we were waiting at traffic lights in Enniskillen. I was looking round at something, when he said urgently, "Go on Dad." I immediately started forward, thinking that the lights had changed, but suddenly realised they were still on red. I slammed on the brakes and stopped clear of the car in front. He roared with laughter, but I told him to never do the like of that again. I could have crashed into the car in front. Shirley took her turn to come with me too. She liked to be helpful, and as we drove along, she would take the invoice from my file, for the next customer. I remember taking her to Franco's for a meal one day as a special treat. She really enjoyed it, but her favourite place was calling at Noel Clarke's of Cornfannog. Like myself, Shirley has a 'sweet tooth,' and Mrs Clarke always gave her a few sweets from the shop. 'Clove rocks' being her favourite.

The smooth running of the mill depended on everyone working as a team, right through from the office girls who took the orders, down to the lorry drivers who did the deliveries. A farmer once told me of a new driver who arrived on his farm with a bulk delivery of dairy nuts. Unfortunately he was doing the evening milking at the time, and the nuts were to be blown up onto the loft over the parlour where the cows were being milked The sound of the nuts being blown in would disturb the cows, so he asked the driver to wait twenty minutes until he had the milking finished. The driver reluctantly agreed and said he had other deliveries to do, and it was getting late. As soon as the farmer had the cows finished he indicated to the driver to go ahead. He connected up the hose and started up the lorry but his patience had expired so he revved up the lorry which in turn increased the blower speed and power. The nuts went up the entry pipe into the loft and were going with such force that they hit the back wall of the loft, and as they built up they forced the corrugated iron roof from the top of the wall and went out through the space and into the cattle collection yard below. Ronnie, (the farmer,) told me he knew the driver was agitated and was aware of him trying to empty the nuts at top speed, but didn't know what had happened until he went out next morning and saw the nuts shattered into powder and lying in the cow manure of the yard. When he rang the mill and told them what had happened, they compensated him for the loss of nuts, and the other nut who had driven the lorry that evening, got paid off at the end of his first week. It seems he was a complete disaster and apart from what I have described, he also delivered feed to wrong farms. He had cost the company a lot by way of compensation in that short time.

The company had a traveller who used to chat too long with his customers, and try to make up the time on the road, with the result that he lost control of his car one day, and the resulting crash killed him. The vacancy was filled by a member of the office staff who wanted to get out and about and meet the customers. After a few months the boss noticed that a previously good customer had a lot of money owing on his account. He rang him up and asked him why he was behind with his account. "I'm not behind with my account, I paid it only last week," was the reply. "Thank you very much," said Mr Smyth, "the problem must be at this end." He called the traveller responsible for this account into his office, and asked him why this particular farmer's account had so much owing. "Well he has bought more land, and is a little tight for money at the moment. I expect he will pay up as soon as he can." Mr Smyth said, "I was speaking to him yesterday and he told me his account was up-to-date." "Do you not believe me Mr Smyth," "No, I don't think I do, how about telling me the truth." He eventually confessed that he had used some money to bet on horses in the hope of making a big win, but had lost the lot, and then used more of the money in the hope of recouping his losses, but he had no luck there either, and was unable to pay the money back. Needless to say Mr Smyth had no option but to give him the sack.

Although the bulk sales brought me in more commission, because I was paid a retainer plus a 'per tonne' commission, I had numerous customers who used bags only. I did a fortnightly run around the north end of the county, in the Derrygonnelly, Kesh, and Belleek areas which were mostly sales of small quantities in bags. However small quantities build up, and helped my overall tonnage count. One couple, who were brother and sister, were very friendly and exact in all their dealings. Each time I arrived they would have the invoice from the last delivery and the exact money to pay it all ready for me. The next question was always an invitation to have a cup of tea. I always accepted, as Stewartie had told me to never refuse a cup of tea as it offends the customer. Sure enough a cup of very strong tea was quickly handed to me by the lady, and as I sipped the tea we talked of current events and retold some tales of what had happened in the past. Usually as the man made a statement his sister would interject with, "Aye surely Robert," or repeat what her brother had just said. I found this amusing and looked forward to my fortnightly visits. I remember he told me one day about a woman who had left her husband and had taken up with another man. To which the sister commented. "Aye!, laying away, Robert." [I think this quote came about when free range hens went away from the farm and made a nest in a distant hedgerow.] However, my visits with them were cut short when the mill received a letter from them, saying they were going to sue, because the lorry had driven past and didn't deliver their feed. They said, "There was a courthouse in Derrygonnelly and another one in Enniskillen, we will sort it out." What had actually happened was that the lorry was a week behind with deliveries and the lorry they saw going past was delivering some feed that had been ordered a week earlier at the cattle market in Enniskillen. Sadly they refused to have anything more to do with Smyths, but we didn't need a courthouse to sort it out.

Another customer was a widow who lived on a very small farm. She used to rear chickens and fatten them up for sale in Derrygonnelly. Her meal bill was small in comparison to other customers, but she was poor and could only pay off her account in very small amounts. The last time I spoke with her she told me she had to go into hospital for some tests. As we spoke I noticed oil running out from her head-scarf and down her face. As she wiped it up with her handkerchief, she remarked, "I have just done my head over with olive oil and some is running down." "That'll keep you from rusting," I said. She was silent for a few moments. Then said, "Keep me from rusting, you're a drole boy." I could hardly believe it when I read her death notice in the local newspaper a few weeks later.

The journey out from Derrygonnelly, and over the mountain, has ruggedly beautiful scenery which is a joy to behold, and I never failed to enjoy it, each time I drove along on my journey towards Garrison, and down into Belleek. I usually reached Belleek about midday and went into the local hotel for something to eat. It was the only place in the small town that served meals.

One day, while I was waiting to be served I got into a chat with a local man, and when I told him I was selling animal feed, he told me a story about a farmer who had a cow badly stuck in a deep drain. The neighbours came to help, and eventually the cow was dragged up onto the bank, but unfortunately, all the pulling and heaving had been too much, and the cow lay there, dead. One neighbour suggested that rather than have a complete loss, why not strip off the pelt and sell it to the local tannery. Thinking this was a good idea, the farmer got a sharp knife and started to cut away the cow's skin. He had just made a long cut down the cow's belly when she jumped to her feet. The pain of the cutting had taken her out of the coma. She wasn't dead after all. What were they to do. They quickly tied her down with the ropes that had been used to pull her out of the drain. Then the farmer cut some young willow saplings from the nearby hedge and pinned them through the skin and along the cut holding it together in the hope that it would heal up with time. The story spread throughout the area, and about three years later a man asked him how the cow that they sewed up with willow rods had done. "Well," says your man, "she did great, healed up nicely and produced a calf and the makings of two creels every year since."

After a six months trial period I was given a company car. It was a Fiat 131. My only car accident occurred with it during my time as a traveller with Smyths. It happened the week before Christmas when I was going round all my customers with the company calendar and the boot full with tins of biscuits which was their Christmas present. I was going towards Rosslea on what I thought was a wet road, when the car started to swing out in the rear as I went round a slow bend in the road. Realising what was happening I took my foot off the throttle and steered into the slide, the car straightened up but went the other direction then. I steered the other way again, and this time the car swung out at the tail as before and continued to go round. Here I was going broadside up the road at about forty miles an hour and unable to do anything about it. Quite a terrifying experience, but got worse as the car went round completely and was now going back-ways and with the slippery road I imagined it had actually increased in speed. As the car was now close to the edge of the road I put on the brakes as tight as I could, hoping to get a grip with the wheels nearest the road edge, where it was very rough. It didn't happen, and the next stage was the back wheel running up the high bank at the side of the road. This dented the back corner and ripped off the exhaust pipe the car went up the bank and eventually rolled over unto its roof. The roll took the car completely across the road. There I was inside the car which was still going back-ways but now on its roof. It eventually stopped. The whole thing happened in less than a minute, but felt much longer, and I was very fortunate that no other traffic was on the road at the time. I was unhurt, and because the car was upside down, I thought it unusual to be winding up the window instead of winding it down, so I could crawl out. The road was like a sheet of glass, I could hardly keep my feet from slipping on it. While I wondered what I should do now, a milk collection lorry came along. The driver stopped and asked if I was okay. I said yes I was, and asked him if he knew where the nearest phone was, so I could get in touch with the police and the mill. "Get in here, I'll take you to the next farm, they have a phone," he said. I walked up the short avenue to the farmhouse, and knocked on the front door. Soon a kindly looking woman appeared, and on hearing my plight asked me in and offered me the use of her phone. I rang the Mill so they could get in touch with the insurance company, then rang the police to explain what had happened. I was afraid of someone else coming along, being unable to stop, and crashing into my upturned car. I finally rang home to tell Gretta. With the phone calls completed I went to thank the lady for the use of the phone, only to find she had made me a cup of tea. I took the tea, thanked her kindly, and set off walking the few hundred yards back to the car. What a surprise I found. The police were there, and the council workers had been along and had spread chips on the road. My car, looking very battered was back on its wheels and was being towed away with a break-down truck back to Lisnaskea. I asked the policeman what had happened to my brief case, calendars, and biscuits. "All that is in the police car and you have to come with us now to Newtownbutler station to make a statement." The policeman listened sympathetically as I unfolded my story, he then wrote out the statement of how I was unaware that there was black ice on the road. I read it through and signed it. That was the last I ever heard of it. The insurance decided to write off the car and in a couple of weeks I had a new car supplied.

After that first winter of high sales, the business settled down and the job became routine, collecting accounts, taking orders, and calling with other farmers in the hope of getting new business. I was just about three years with the company when they were taken over by Wilson's Feeds of Belfast. Wilson's Feeds had just put up a new mill and was running a very efficient operation. Apart from the office staff, they had just three men running the actual plant as it was mostly automatic. This was a big contrast to Smyth's where they employed about forty men and were only turning out a fraction of the tonnage of the Wilson plant. Wilson's was managed by Brian Lyons, he had the sharpest brain of anyone I have ever met - even yet. No matter what was said to him, he had an immediate answer, he didn't seem to need thinking time. During my first chat with him, I found I needed to use all my brain power with deep concentration to keep up with him. But I developed a technique of my own for dealing with him. If ever I had to approach him with a problem, I would consider what all possible answers he could give me, and then I had my response ready. Once I put in an order for three tonnes of nuts, but when the lorry arrived at the farm it had six tonnes on it. The farmer didn't have room to handle that amount. The balance left on the lorry had to be taken to a stone quarry, where there was a weigh-bridge suitable for weighing lorries, so the surplus amount could be weighed and deducted from the account. On this occasion the amount returned didn't tally with what the farmer was billed for, so a balance of around one hundred pounds had to be written off. Brian phoned me up to see why this man had got the money off his bill. I said, "I'll tell you the story." He stopped me at once. "I don't want to hear any story, tell me what happened." After listening to my explanation he said, "This is a one off situation, we can't afford this kind of pay out." To which I replied, "Just dispatch the correct amount and it will never happen again."

Wilson's, being a larger company, had salesmen in all six counties of Northern Ireland. We met up every quarter for a new product launch, or a meeting to see where more business was to be had. My immediate boss was a man called Irvine Hamill. Irvine was a shrewd business man, and often came down to Fermanagh to do a day out with me in the hope of getting more business. He also owned a fleet of lorries which were employed by the company to deliver the orders. During my time with Wilson's feeds, Irvine saw a good business opportunity, and bought a pig processing factory near by where he lived. So we had a farewell present and party for him at the mill one day. My job continued as before, sometimes everything running smoothly along, and at other times a complete nightmare. Complaints about the nuts breaking down into powder and then complaints about the nuts sticking in the bins and hoppers, other travellers canvassing them with keen prices or orders not delivered on time, and farmers ringing me up to say their nuts had run completely out. When such a phone call came through, it was then an emergency delivery, to get the feed to him before the next milking time. I asked a farmer one time. "Did you not know your supply of nuts were getting low?" "Of course I did," he replied, "when I opened the chute and nothing came out." Another time the lorry was delivering to a new customer near Roslea, and the driver found the narrow lane had a bridge set at an angle over a small river.

He realised that to go through he would pull the front mudguard off the lorry on the corner of the bridge, so he phoned back to the mill and explained his problem. He was told to go on through and take the chance. Sure enough the corner of the bridge ripped the mudguard off, but he got to the farm and delivered the feed okay. Then on the way out, he took off the mudguard from the other side.

As one gets to know each farmer better, and listen to his problems each time the farm is visited, a picture begins to build up of the type of character he is. One young farmer told me he had worked for the previous owner from the day he left school, and when he died he bequeathed the farm to him. When I first started calling with him, the farm was in good structural shape, with signs of a lot of new building work having been done in recent years, but he did some unusual things. After two or three visits he asked me to not call at milking time. Now I had left Enniskillen around nine am, and called with farmers along my route, arriving with Paddy about eleven thirty. "You seem to milk the cows very late in the morning," I said, to which he replied, "Well you see Robert, I watch television until it closes down about midnight, and then I do the milking, so the cows aren't ready for a morning milking until this time of day." He had the lane up to the farm newly done with concrete, and I mentioned how it was such a good job. He said, "You know Robert, I ordered up three thousand pounds worth of concrete for that job, when I hadn't the price of a four course dinner in my pocket." He called in a local contractor one year to cut the silage for him. They arrived one morning with a team of men and a fleet of tractors and equipment to do the job. Paddy was operating his tractor and buckrake to pack each trailer load of chopped grass into the silage pit, but the loads were coming so fast that Paddy couldn't keep pace with it. Soon the yard by the silage pit was full of dumped grass and then they filled up the area around the dwelling house, front and back, and ended up with some down the entrance lane as well. Before leaving that night the contractor asked Paddy if they would give him a miss the next day so he could get all the grass cleared up. "Not at all," says Paddy, "you come back tomorrow, I'll have it cleared up." Paddy worked all night, and was scooping up the last of the grass when the team arrived the next morning.

There was a lovely family who had a small farm, near Rosslea, and a cup of tea was always given to me on my arrival there. The father was retired and was a joy to listen to, as he told me story after story. I had to excuse myself and say, "I can't stay much longer because I have a lot more calls to do," and proceed on my way. One day he told me about a local man who was always bragging about how straight his potato ridges were. So one night a couple of young lads got a bucket of lime wash, and painted it along the edge of each of his ridges. He said, "Everyone could admire the straightness of the ridges from miles away after that, until the growth of the tops, covered them in." He told of another man who had had a religious conversion. He was so convinced of the power of prayer, that he said to one of his neighbours. "If you had genuine belief in God and prayed strongly for something, God would bring it about for you, he could even bring up potatoes in your garden without you planting them at all." The neighbour told what he had heard in the local pub, and one night someone slipped in quietly into his garden and planted a few potatoes.

When the potatoes appeared in the garden, the preacher was amazed, and my storyteller said, "He preached 'a tarra' after that." (with conviction) Another day he told me of a headstone that was in the local St Tirney's Churchyard at Rosslea. The epitaph read as follows;

Dear friend, as you pass by,

as you are now, so once was I.

As I am now, so you will be,

prepare yourself, to follow me.

Underneath, some local wit had written in chalk.

To follow you I'd be content,

If I only knew which way you went.

I decided to take a look at this headstone, and sure enough, it was there just as he had described it to me, but the chalk sequel had disappeared.

Another farmer was so laid back that I don't know how he made any profit at all. He appeared to take the attitude that if it wasn't done today, sure it could be done tomorrow, or even next week. His cattle yard was covered in a couple of inches of cow dung, and if I arrived when he was doing the morning milking, which in his case was about ten thirty in the morning, he would come out of the byre, leaving the cows with the milking machines on them, and come over to the yard gate to me where I was marooned on the clean side, and talk for about ten minutes, eventually saying, "I suppose I better get you the cheque book." There was no hurry whatsoever as he talked on for another ten or fifteen minutes after we had the transaction completed, usually finishing by saying, "I better get back to the cows, I have a few more to milk." Having farmed myself and knowing that four or five minutes is enough time to milk a cow. I wondered how his poor cows survived a half hour with the vacuum of the machine sucking away on their teats long after all the milk had gone. He didn't seem to care less, just plodded on in his own carefree way. But then one wonders who has got it right. Is it the fellow who strives to make as much money as he can, so he can have a big house, fancy car, holidays abroad, and drives himself on relentlessly to achieve it, or is it the fellow who is happy to sit on a grassy bank and watch a bumble bee hovering around the fragrant blooms of a gorse bush. From the cradle to the grave, sure 'It's Only a Matter of Time.'

About the Author

Robert Montgomery was born and reared on a farm in the townland of Derrygiff, near Enniskillen. At the age of thirty two he emigrated to Western Australia with his wife Gretta and three children, Gordon, Kenneth, and Shirley. He includes his experiences in Ireland and then in Australia as a young man. He also recounts his career on returning to Ireland, in the retail trade, and later as an animal feed salesman. Now retired, he lives near his family in Cheltenham, Gloucestershire, England.

Lightning Source UK Ltd.
Milton Keynes UK
23 November 2009

146629UK00001B/13/P